OPPOSITIONAL DEFIANT DISORDER

A Cutting-Edge Method for Recognizing and Guiding Your O.D.D Child Towards Success (2022 Guide for Beginners)

Darlene Ramos

Table of Content

Chapter 10: Medication and Treatment, Therapies of Various Types

Here are some interesting concepts related to family therapy:

Introduction

Disruptive behaviour includes negative, aggressive, and defiant behaviour toward authority figures such as parents or teachers. The symptoms typically begin in childhood but can persist into adulthood.

People with ODD may be easily irritated, argue with teachers and authority figures, or have difficulty taking turns in games. They may disobey rules, purposefully annoy others, or refuse to play by the rules of a game. Children with ODD are frequently dissatisfied with their schools and teachers, and they may struggle to adjust to changes in their environment. Rather than direct disobedience to authority figures, there may be a pattern of rebellious behaviour such as truancy, getting into fights, fleeing from home, or being uncooperative and difficult at school. They may exhibit problems with behaviour such as lying, stealing, bullying others, or vandalizing property that does not usually involve violence. Children and teenagers with ODD may also struggle with low self-esteem, a lack of motivation in school, or boredom with their activities such as sports or hobbies. Separation anxiety, temper tantrums, and bedwetting are common symptoms in young children. Parents or teachers may ignore or criticize the children's behaviour, fueling their rage and hostility.

Children with ODD are more likely to engage in other types of offending, such as bullying or truancy, as well as get into trouble with the police or the law. They may also have academic issues, such as poor grades or poor attendance. ODD symptoms can impair their ability to function socially, leading to social isolation and withdrawal. Some children feel shame and embarrassment because they fear being judged negatively by others because of their behaviour. Children with ODD may also have attention deficit hyperactivity disorder, anxiety, or depression. Adults are also at a higher risk of developing an antisocial personality disorder.

ODD in children is typically treated by a psychiatrist or psychologist. The treatment involves teaching the child how to control their anger and improve their social skills in stressful situations by learning behavioural techniques. Positive reinforcement for good behaviour, such as rewards for staying at home without getting into trouble, or positive feedback for completing tasks and meeting goals, are examples of these techniques. Parents are also taught to reward good behaviour and create schedules to help their children effectively schedule their time throughout the day, including homework time and rest time. In some cases, these behavioural techniques are used in conjunction with medication to treat ODD.

Problem-solving techniques and self-help skills are also taught to children with ODD in order to improve their social relationships, schoolwork, physical health, stress management, and organisation. Children in these programmes are taught how to calm themselves down when they are angry, rather than allowing this to lead to worse behaviour, through work with a psychologist or psychiatrist. The treatment can last anywhere between six months and a year.

ODD differs from other disorders in that it is characterized by aggressive behaviour toward others and rebellion against authority figures such as parents or teachers. ODD is frequently seen in children who also have other disruptive behavioural disorders, such as conduct disorder and attention deficit hyperactivity disorder. Children with ODD frequently engage in behaviours such as lying, stealing, bullying, or vandalizing property, or failing to follow the rules of nonviolent games. These behaviours may result in academic difficulties or problems with peers, such as fighting.

One of the most important things to remember when trying to distinguish between ODD and ADHD is that, despite their similarities, they are two distinct disorders. The distinction between the two is that ODD children are primarily angry and argumentative, whereas ADHD children may not be angry but exhibit hyperactive behaviour, move around a lot, and are easily distracted by their surroundings.

Chapter 1
What Exactly Is ODD?

You may believe that your child's rebellious behaviour is normal when they are young; after all, toddlers are notorious for demanding and challenging behavior. What are your first thoughts supposed to be as they get older and this type of behaviour does not diminish? Every child and adolescent displays defiance, disrespect for rules and authority figures, and vindictiveness from time to time. Children are more likely to throw tantrums, whereas teenagers are snotty, irritable, and extremely moody. When this behaviour is applied to Oppositional Defiant Disorder, children and teenagers' behaviour becomes excessive and destructive, causing havoc in the child's personal life or at school.

Before defining Oppositional Defiant Disorder, it is important to differentiate between Oppositional Defiant Behavior, which is present in all teenagers and children, and when it manifests as Oppositional Defiant Disorder or ODD. Oppositional Defiant Disorder (ODD) is best described as a repetitive emotive pattern that has lasted at least six months to indicate that it is not an acute emotional outburst or an emotional issue that the child or teen has had to deal with that is not typically associated with a chronic condition. It is also aimed specifically at authority figures in the child or teen's life, such as parents, coaches, or educators. Normally, there is no aggression involved because this behaviour would indicate another problem known as conduct disorder. ODD is typically verbal and not physically manifested. Aside from the fact that their manifestation should be continued for a period of six months or longer, there is a list of symptoms that a child must be associated with for a possible diagnosis. Another feature that distinguishes an ODD child or teen from a normal child is that nothing seems to satisfy the child or teen's dissatisfaction or disdain for authority, authority figures, and nothing seems to make them happy.

Children under the age of five are known to exhibit defiant and argumentative behaviour on a regular or even daily basis; in an older child, it may occur at least twice a week. The main goal is to try to identify a pattern of behaviour that is more intense and indicates a frequency that appears abnormal and has a high-intensity level when compared to typical child behavior. A functional way to measure the level of intensity of the child or teen's behavior is by looking for areas in their lives where this behaviour is causing damage or impairment. For example, this ongoing tendency from your child or teen to cause conflict and object to authority may possibly make things very difficult at home. It can also lead to a variety of issues in school, including poor academic performance, social alienation, and the loss of friends. It is not uncommon for children or teenagers with ODD to become socially marginalized in environments like school. Although there is an estimate that about 3% of children suffer from ODD, medical professionals add that there is a strong possibility that the number is actually higher due to the fact that there may be many children and teenagers who have not been diagnosed with the condition.

The Physiological Development Research has been conducted on the neurological aspects of children and teenagers who are diagnosed with ODD, and although no hard evidence was found, an open question remains among specialists about some neurobiological differences between children diagnosed with ODD and those who are not. An interesting research based observation postulates that ODD is more prevalent in boys than in girls, only prior to the onset of puberty. However, after the onset of puberty, the number of cases starts to even out between the sexes, with ODD affecting 9% of girls and 11% of boys. It is also said that the way symptoms are displayed is different between the sexes, which may be relevant to the general ways young girls and boys approach and handle different situations.

There are studies indicating that some factors can make specific children more susceptible or likely to develop ODD than others. One of these factors that play a role in how likely a child or teen is to develop ODD or other conduct disorders is a genetic component. An interesting link is made between individuals diagnosed with mood disorders, ADHD, antisocial personality, and substance abuse disorders, and the likelihood of a first-degree relative (children) developing ODD. These are the physiological and neurological components of ODD that have thus far been discovered, but also in existence is a strong nature versus nurture argument which postulates that the manifestation of ODD occurs due to an interplay between genes and the environment the child or teenager is in.

There is some encouraging news in statistical data, though, as an estimated two-thirds of children diagnosed with ODD will be able to deal with and overcome their destructive symptoms and behavior, and when a child who is diagnosed with Oppositional Defiant Disorder reaches the age of 17, there is a 70% chance that this disorder will no longer be playing a dominating role in their life and that they will not be experiencing any symptoms of ODD.

Symptoms and Behavior

There are specific symptoms a parent should be on the lookout for if they suspect that their child or teenager may suffer from ODD. This list is lengthy, but the child does not have to exhibit symptoms of all of the listed symptoms; as previously stated, only four symptoms are required for a probable diagnosis. The symptoms on the list include situations in which a child or teenager frequently loses their temper or is annoyed and touchy for no apparent reason. These children also have resentful attitudes and behaviours, and they are frequently irritated by authority figures or situations in which they must follow rules.

ODD symptoms also include a hostile and argumentative attitude toward any figure they perceive to be an authority figure, and if an authority figure makes a request, the child or teen will not comply, especially if the request is related to rules or adhering to rules. These are also possible symptoms if your child or teen goes out of their way to intentionally annoy others and refuses to accept responsibility for their mistakes. When they get into trouble or are the focus of a disciplinary process, ODD children and teens are known for blaming others. Finally, a concerned parent should be on the lookout for spiteful and vindictive behaviour.

These behaviours do not necessarily occur frequently; however, if you have observed them within the last six months, you can include them as a valid behavioural symptom. This diagnostic manual is based on the Diagnostic and Statistical Manual of Mental Disorders published by the American Psychiatric Association (DSM-5). Parents should remember that ODD symptoms vary from person to person, so if you know someone whose child has ODD and they behave in a certain way, try not to use the child as your parameter; instead, use the provided set of symptoms.

We are all unique, and when it comes to mental disorders, we may have the same problem but exhibit very different symptoms.

Especially in a case like this, where a child or adolescent only requires four of the eight main symptoms for an initial consultation, different children with ODD's behaviour can be very similar but also very different. Keep your child's personality and temperament in mind when looking for these symptoms in your child to ensure that you identify the symptoms authentically and contextually. Some common cognitive symptoms of ODD include a child or adolescent's inability to speak before thinking, difficulty concentrating, and frequent bouts of frustration (Valley Behavioral Health System, 2017; Mayo Clinic, 2018).

Causes, Risk Factors, and Related Disorders

Co-occurring disorders must also be discussed because they may be a precursor or an indication that a child is more likely to develop oddly. The child does not have to have one of these conditions, but they may have a close relative who does. Conditions or disorders that typically manifest later in life, such as bipolar disorder, are more likely to occur in children or teens who exhibit symptoms of ODD. When evaluating a child or adolescent with ODD, it is critical to look for signs of other co-occurring disorders. Attention deficit hyperactivity disorder (ADHD), learning disabilities, depression, bipolar disorder (as previously mentioned), and anxiety disorders are among these conditions. If a coexisting condition can be identified and treated alongside the ODD symptoms, the treatment may be significantly more successful, as these coexisting conditions frequently aggravate ODD in a child or adolescent, causing even more difficulty, confusion, and frustration. There have also been reports of children and teens diagnosed with ODD developing conduct disorder, in which the child develops a pattern of violent and disruptive rebellious behavior. To comprehend ODD as a whole, one must also comprehend which other conditions a child or adolescent may have that can aggravate the symptoms.

Anxiety Illness

Although anxiety is normal in a stressful situation, having anxiety disorder refers to a situation in which someone experiences this state of angst or fear to such an extent that it affects their well-being and ability to live a normal life. A physiological anxiety response occurs when your brain detects a threat and responds by secreting hormones that put your body on guard. Children and teenagers can become anxious at school if they have to prepare for a big test while they haven't done their homework and the teacher is busy checking everyone's work, if they are waiting for test results, or if they have relationship insecurity with their friends.

They may also experience anxiety at home if there is a conflict between parents or siblings, if their living situation is unstable, or if they are experiencing significant financial difficulties. However, all of these are normal, albeit serious, reasons for a child to be anxious.

When someone suffers from an anxiety disorder, they may experience the same situations, but their level of anxiety is so high that they become overwhelmed. A child or adolescent with an anxiety disorder is constantly afraid and anxious, which causes them to avoid normal activities such as going to school, socializing with friends, avoiding situations where you need to go out in public because they don't want to face other people, and limiting communication with others, including family.

Several types of anxiety disorders have been identified as a result of extensive research on the subject, which may apply to younger individuals who may also have ODD. First, there is Generalized Anxiety Disorder, which is defined as an excessive and unrealistic feeling of worry for what is normally perceived as a situation that does not necessitate that level of worry.

Then there's panic disorder, which includes feelings of anxiety and excessive worry but is also distinguished by sudden feelings of overwhelming fear and panic, resulting in a panic attack. During a panic attack, a person may experience palpitations, chest pain, difficulty breathing, as well as perspiration. They are terrified, and this disorients them from their immediate surroundings and reality. The severity of this experience may occasionally cause the individual to feel as if they are having a heart attack or that they are unable to inhale enough oxygen, resulting in a choking sensation.

When you spend a lot of time premeditating and then worrying about everyday social situations, you have a social anxiety disorder, also known as social phobia. For example, from the perspective of a child or adolescent, they will likely imagine the worst social outcome for them, which would most likely result in embarrassment or shame, and then obsessively worry about it. Separation anxiety is a common type of anxiety that affects children, but it can affect anyone. When one of a child's parents dies, especially when they are young, they may experience separation anxiety because they are afraid of losing their other parent or any other family member. Although such fear has some validity, especially after losing someone close to you, some people have an irrational fear when someone they love leaves or is not in their direct sight or contact.

Additionally, anxiety can be caused by certain prescription medications, so if your child is taking medication, talk to your doctor about the side effects and whether the medication is causing unnecessary anxiety that could be exacerbating a condition like ODD. Anxiety is not a one-size-fits-all concept or condition, so when you're looking for signs of increased anxiety in your child's behavior, keep these different types in mind (Lerche Davis, 2003).

Disorders of Depression

Disruptive mood dysregulation disorder, major depressive disorder, and persistent depressive disorder or dysthymia are the three major types of depressive disorders commonly diagnosed in children and adolescents. In general, the term "depression" is overused and can be used to describe feelings or experiences that have nothing to do with actual depressive disorders.

Everyone, adults and children alike, have times when they feel down, which are most likely caused by events in their daily lives. When a person does not have a depressive disorder, this sensation of being 'down' goes away, and it is not considered the person's normal state of mind. For example, the term "depression" or "feeling depressed" is frequently used to describe a person's discouragement as a result of a traumatic event that resulted in disappointment or loss. Depressive disorders are characterized by a pattern of low mood levels that are linked to feelings of worthlessness and self-loathing. Depression in children is thought to be caused by the same thing that causes depression in adults: a significant loss or deprivation early in life.

Children with depressive disorders may not be able to articulate their emotional experiences as well as adults, but when observed, these children or teens will most likely exhibit poor academic performance, attempts to withdraw from society, and may even act out in a delinquent manner. Children and teenagers who have a depressive disorder will appear irritable or aggressive rather than sad, which is a significant difference between adult and childhood depression. Children and teenagers suffering from depressive disorders may exhibit overactive, aggressive, and antisocial behavior.

To begin, disruptive mood dysregulation disorder is characterized by disruptive behaviour and persistent irritability in children between the ages of 6 and 10 years. Because their behavioural symptoms are so similar, this type of depressive disorder is closely related to ODD. ADHD and anxiety are also associated with disruptive mood dysregulation disorder. This type of depressive disorder can be diagnosed after the age of six or before the age of eighteen. When a patient reaches adulthood, this condition may progress to unipolar disorder, which consists of depression with no signs of mania or anxiety disorder. Always seek the advice of a medical professional before attempting to diagnose your child with any condition, but disruptive mood dysregulation disorder usually necessitates a combination of behaviours occurring simultaneously for 12 months with no gaps of three months.

This is something that can be observed in the absence of a doctor. These behaviours are, first and foremost, aggressive outbursts that are disproportionate to the relevant situation and can manifest in verbal and physical expressions of rage (these will most likely occur three times per week on average), and the child will also exhibit temper-based outbursts that appear to be inconsistent with the level of cognitive and emotional development for their age, and appearing angry and irritable most of the time. It is also critical that the child's outbursts be observed in two of the three settings in which they find themselves on a daily basis: school, home, or in the presence of their peers.

Although it can occur at any age, major depressive disorder is more common after puberty. This type of depressive disorder differs from disruptive mood deregulation disorder in that it is characterized by a two-week-long depressive episode. Remission may occur within 6-12 months if the disorder is not treated.

Children and teenagers who have had severe episodes, children who have had an episode at a younger age, and children who have had multiple depressive episodes are at a higher risk of recurrence. Signs of major depressive disorder can be identified if a child, first, feels sad or even tearful almost every day for two weeks, and second, if the child loses interest in things they would normally enjoy doing, which can appear as an expression of high-level boredom.

Along with these two main indicators, you may notice symptoms such as insomnia or hypersomnia, weight changes, which are most commonly recorded as decreased weight in children, fatigue, difficulty concentrating, possible recurrent thoughts about death or suicide, and feelings of worthlessness or rejection or disapproval.

Even a child experiencing inappropriate guilt in the context can be an indicator. Major depressive disorder in adolescent children can have devastating consequences such as academic decline, substance abuse, and suicidal ideation. Major depression in children and teenagers can cause them to fall behind academically and miss out on important relationships with their peers.

Persistent depressive disorder, also known as dysthymia, is defined as a persistently irritable or depressed mood that lasts most of the day on most days for more than a year. At least two of the following behavioural symptoms are also present: feelings of hopelessness, insomnia or hypersomnia, fatigue, difficulty concentrating, low self-esteem, and either a decreased appetite or overeating.

A clinical diagnosis is required for all of these types of depressive disorders that can manifest in childhood and adolescence. However, it is impossible to ignore how closely some of these types of depressive disorders, which are also considered possible co-occurring disorders, resemble symptoms of ODD. Most types, for example, indicate irritable behaviour, and the first type we discussed, disruptive mood deregulation disorder, includes symptoms such as aggression and behaviour that can interfere with their social development.

This could be why these disorders co-occur, and the potential influence and aggravating factors they may have on ODD should be investigated so that parents can have clarity on the subject. Let's start with another disorder that typically manifests itself in young adulthood, but has also been diagnosed and studied in children and teenagers (Coryell, 2020).

Bipolar Illness

Bipolar disorder frequently begins as a major depressive disorder in children, and symptoms of bipolar disorder can appear between the ages of puberty and the mid-twenties. Even though a type of depressive disorder is a precursor to bipolar disorder, it is important to note that not all children with one will develop bipolar disorder. Although bipolar disorder is an important component of a legitimate co-occurring disorder of ODD, it is not very common in children. Previous diagnoses of prepubescent children with intensely unstable moods were bipolar disorder, but this diagnosis has been changed to disruptive mood dysregulation disorder due to the condition typically progressing in the direction of a depressive disorder rather than a subsequent, fully-blown bipolar disorder as the child grows older. Bipolar disorder may develop after puberty in the young adulthood of an individual who had ODD as a child and can thus be linked to ODD.

From a behavioral or symptomatic standpoint, Bipolar Disorder is distinguished by periods of mania, depression, and what appears to be a "normal mood." The requirement for diagnosis is that these states alternate and reoccur frequently and can last for weeks or months before transitioning to another state or mood. Bipolar Disorder is typically treated with psychiatric drugs, but therapy is also recommended.

There is no concrete evidence about what causes bipolar disorder, but medical experts and researchers believe that there is a genetic or hereditary component, as well as dysregulation of the neurotransmitters norepinephrine and serotonin and that a stressful life event is a likely contributing factor.

When an adolescent is going through a manic phase or episode, they may appear very positive or even hyperirritable, and these moods can also alternate. They tend to go into productivity mode, and their speech is noticeably quick and driven. Their sleep patterns will change as they begin to sleep less, and they will develop an inflated self-esteem or a grandiose self-perception. Mania can progress to psychosis, in which the adolescent loses touch with reality and claims to be God, to have supreme knowledge that no one else has, and to have a severely impaired sense of judgment, which leads to reckless and self-destructive behaviour such as casual sex, binge drinking, and even drug abuse. Because of the serious consequences that a manic episode can have on an adolescent's life, it is critical to monitor the situation and seek professional help. If your young child has ODD, you don't have to worry about them developing the bipolar disorder as they get older; however, if you're aware of the disorder's prevalence in relatives, you can help your child by conducting some preventive behavioural observation.

IED (Intermittent Explosive Disorder)

The intermittent explosive disorder is defined by extreme and aggressive outbursts that can include impulsive, violent behaviour and verbal outbursts that do not fit the context of the situation at all. It is usually perceived as a massive overreaction that is completely out of proportion to the situation. Examples of intermittent explosive disorder in adults include road rage, domestic abuse, attempting to throw or break objects in your vicinity, and extreme temper tantrums. The disorder is classified as chronic, and a child may exhibit symptoms for years, though the severity of the episodes or outbursts will decrease as the individual grows older.

The symptoms of the intermittent explosive disorder can be frightening for someone who has never had an outburst like this before. A completely genuine episode can develop and erupt within 30 minutes, completely unexpectedly.

This disorder is more difficult to diagnose because these outbursts can be separated by weeks or even months of non-violent and non-aggressive behaviour, giving the appearance of an isolated incident. It is also possible that the main outbursts are physically aggressive and are interspersed with verbal outbursts that appear less serious. A person suffering from the intermittent explosive disorder may be chronically angry, irritable, and impulsive.

A tight feeling in the chest, tremors, and palpitations, a tingling sensation under the skin, a sudden surge of energy, racing thoughts, and rage or irritability can accompany or precede an outburst or episode. Has your child ever displayed any of these symptoms? Shouting, temper tantrums, heated arguments, shoving or slapping others, vandalism or causing property damage, and threats to harm people or animals are common accompanying verbal and physical outbursts. After the episode or outburst has ended, the child or individual may feel relieved and physically exhausted. Later on, they will feel shame, remorse, guilt, regret, or embarrassment.

There are several causes of the intermittent explosive disorder, and they can interact with one another. This means that the disorder is rarely caused by a single factor. The first factor that can cause intermittent explosive disorder is genetics, as with most disorders. When it comes to mental disorders, genetics are not often ruled out as a causal factor, and if there is a family member, specifically a direct family member, who has also shown symptoms or received a diagnosis for this specific disorder, this is a valid reason to keep your eyes peeled.

The environment is another frequently present contributing factor.

Because environmental factors cannot be completely ruled out when investigating the cause of mental illness, they will always be a potential causal component. However, specific environmental circumstances, such as physical and verbal abuse, are isolated and emphasized in this case.

Early exposure to this type of harmful behavior can set off the intermittent explosive disorder. Finally, differences in brain function, chemistry, and structure can cause a child to develop intermittent explosive disorder. This statement is based solely on observations, and while the concept is entirely plausible, concrete evidence has yet to be produced. Finally, two risk factors associated with these causes give you reason to be concerned as a parent of a child with this disorder. They are, first and foremost, if the child has been subjected to physical abuse, and secondly if the child has been diagnosed with or exhibits symptoms of other mental disorders.

Children with intermittent explosive disorder will eventually struggle to form meaningful relationships, will experience inconsistencies and mood problems, and will face difficulties at school and home as a result. If the condition is not treated, they may self-harm and develop other health problems such as diabetes, heart problems, high blood pressure, and physical pain (Mayo Clinic, 2020).

Intellectual Developmental Disabilities

Intellectual developmental disorder, also known as IDD, is a neuro-developmental disorder that was recently discovered and labeled, where the symptoms and characteristics were previously classified as "mental retardation." However, because IDD is not a complete manifestation of mental disability, it was given its own identity and is now classified as a mental disorder.

The key components of the intellectual developmental disorder are associated with a child's developmental deficits or shortcomings in specific intellectual processes and intellectual functioning. These functions include proper reasoning, effective judgment, planning, abstract thinking, and general learning difficulties.

The learning processes of a child with IDD are noticeably slower than those of a child with no such impairments. This disorder's signs and symptoms can be seen at various stages of a child's development. Children with IDD, for example, may have difficulty crawling and standing up, and they may do so much later than other children. Their vocal abilities are also likely to develop later, and once they are old enough to attend school, problems may arise in the classroom due to their difficulty with clear communication and interpreting and applying new information that is presented to them.

Because of their slower processing of information and inability to understand some concepts, a child with IDD will struggle to keep up with their peers in school. They will not be able to develop problem-solving skills, for example, and may show a lack of social inhibitions or an understanding of how social norms work. In this case, however, they do so because they do not understand social boundaries, as opposed to a rebellious child crossing social boundaries on purpose. A child with IDD may struggle with everyday tasks that other children consider completely normal, such as giving someone the correct change, following cooking instructions, or organizing pantry items.

Genes or genetic syndromes, malformations in the child's brain, the influence of drugs or alcohol during pregnancy, traumatic brain injury, complications during labor, types of seizure disorders, and even severe social deprivation are all risk factors for IDD. An IQ test is used to diagnose IDD, and a score of less than 70 indicates that the child may have IDD. This IQ score, however, is insufficient for a comprehensive diagnosis; the child must be observed to determine whether there are any other adaptive or communication issues present. Except if the child suffers physical trauma or a toxic exposure before reaching the age of 18, it is assumed that this disorder exists before birth (Child Mind Institute, 2020a).

Language Impairment

Children with language disorders typically struggle with both understanding and speaking a language, which is usually their native language. Language disorder and speech sound disorder are not the same thing; however, the two can be confused. Speech sound disorder is characterized by problematic sound production.

Language disorder is a communication disorder in which a child has ongoing difficulties with language use as well as language acquisition. A child, for example, may struggle to process specific linguistic information such as sentence structure, vocabulary, and discourse. The disorder interferes with a child's ability to process and produce language, as well as forms of communication, whether spoken, written, or gestural. Children with language disorders, on the other hand, have no trouble producing speech sounds.

If your child has a language disorder, symptoms will most likely have appeared from an early age; however, you will not be aware of this until their functioning requires more complex linguistic processing. A child with a language disorder will typically struggle to comprehend and process what others say, especially when compared to the speed of comprehension of a child who does not have a language disorder.

This disorder can cause the child to leave out words from a sentence when speaking, to frequently use placeholders like 'um' while searching for words when speaking, and to frequently repeat or echo parts of questions, whole questions, and incorrect tenses. These kids appear shy because they are hesitant to speak because it is a difficult process for them.

If your family or ancestors have a history of language disorders, you should be on the lookout for signs and symptoms. A diagnosis requires that a child have communication problems or deficits that are deemed appropriate for their age, affecting their vocabulary, sentence structure, and if they have difficulty using the correct language to transfer information in a conversation. Speech therapy is the most effective treatment for language disorders, and it can be combined with cognitive behaviour therapy and psychotherapy (Child Mind Institute, 2020b).

Disorder of Conduct

Oppositional defiant disorder is frequently confused with conduct disorder. However, if you look at the symptoms, you'll notice some startling differences that will make you wonder why you ever compared them in the first place. Nonetheless, knowing what conduct disorder is will help you understand the symptoms of your child's ODD. Here is a list of the most common conduct disorder symptoms, inclinations, and behaviours in children.

Conduct disorder or its prevalence affects approximately 10% of children, with symptoms most commonly manifesting in late childhood to early adolescence. This disorder is also more common in boys than in girls, and it differs from oppositional defiant disorder in that it exhibits significantly more violent behaviour. Conduct disorder is defined as a pattern of persistent or recurring behaviour that violates the rights of others while also violating age-appropriate societal norms or rules.

Although genetics cannot be ruled out as a factor in the development of this disorder, a strong emphasis is placed on the child's home environment, and if a child's parents regularly engage in substance abuse or have been diagnosed with disorders such as schizophrenia, ADHD, mood disorders, or an antisocial personality disorder, this can be a strong indicator of the cause of conduct disorder development. Having said that, it is not unheard of for a child to develop conduct disorder while growing up in what appears to be a healthy and well-functioning household. So, what distinguishes conduct disorder from oppositional defiant disorder (ODD)? Here are some indicators to look for, though I doubt you'd have to look too hard.

A child with conduct disorder lacks the ability to empathize with others in terms of their well-being and emotions, and they can easily interpret another child's or adult's behaviour as intentionally threatening even when there are no signs of a threat.

Children with conduct disorder want to cause harm and do so by acting aggressively, bullying others, committing acts of physical cruelty on others, displaying and using weapons, forcing another to participate in a sexual act, and showing no regret or remorse for their actions. They are likely to direct their rage and cruelty toward animals, and they have no qualms about lying, stealing, or vandalising property. They do not tolerate rules and are more likely to flee from home or school.

Although boys are more likely than girls to have conduct disorder, there is a significant difference in their symptoms that can be useful to know. On the one hand, boys are more likely to vandalise, steal, and fight, indicating a problem with physical conduct. Girls, on the other hand, are more likely to run away from home, tell lies, and become involved in prostitution. Both sexes are likely to use illegal drugs and have suicidal thoughts. Suicidal tendencies or suicide attempts must be taken very seriously in these cases (Elia, 2019).

Complications

Undiagnosed and untreated ODD has serious consequences that can have a long-term impact on your child's life. Early detection, while not always possible due to the six-month time span required for the detection of any legitimate initial signs, is critical for the child's or teen's well-being because, as the condition worsens, it can lead to serious complications in their lives that can last until adulthood. These complications include social issues such as the loss or complete lack of friendships and close relationships, as well as the subsequent inability to develop any sort of meaningful relationships. They may go through life experiencing social isolation, and while they may attend an educational institution, this setting will most likely be difficult for them to adjust to and function in.

If ODD is not treated and the child or adolescent grows into adulthood, issues may persist and even worsen.

Such an individual, for example, would show an ongoing pattern of broken relationships and relationship conflicts; they would typically try to control those around them, which is one of the causes of their social alienation and isolation. Another factor is an individual's inability to let go of a grudge or to forgive someone, which can completely destroy a relationship. When these defiant children grow up, they still don't get along with authority figures, which may cost them their jobs or land them in jail (Valley Behavioral Health System, 2017; Mayo Clinic, 2018).

How to Deal with Information Overload

Starting with the main topic of discussion, oppositional defiant disorder, and then moving on to a lengthy discussion of potential co-occurring conditions or disorders that are or have been associated with ODD, this chapter has provided a wealth of information about mental disorders. So, as concerned parents, what should we make of all this information? Some of the symptoms discussed in a few co-occurring conditions, such as mood disorders and intermittent explosive disorder, can be downright terrifying, making you fear for your child's health and sanity.

The purpose of the first chapter, on the other hand, is to lay out all of the facts about ODD so that the rest of the guide can proceed based on information. This chapter is synonymous with the adage "knowledge is power," and it aims to provide you with the most up-to-date information available to you and your child.

When it comes to these details, there is one golden rule that every parent should follow. We are all aware of how protective we are of our children. Mixing knowledge or information with emotion, or worse, paranoia or neuroticism, is not a good idea. Chapter 1 is your toolbox, where you can learn more about the various components that may contribute to your child's condition. However, it is critical that you do not diagnose your child based on this information; if you know your child has ODD but suspect that another disorder is lurking in the background, the best thing you can do for your child is to take them to a therapist or psychiatrist and tell the medical professional about your observations. Everything you've read thus far has given you a sense of empowerment. In the following chapter, we'll look at you, your power as a human being, and how you can use your strength to benefit your entire family.

When Is Oppositional Defiant Disorder Diagnosed?

ODD is difficult to diagnose because it frequently overlaps with other developmental disorders or mental health issues.

As a result, it can be difficult to determine which manifestations are solely caused by oppositional defiant disorder.

As a general rule, an oppositional defiant disorder diagnosis can be made around the age of four. It is normal for children to exhibit oppositional and defiant behaviours up to the age of three. They are seeking independence, learning the value of saying "no," and pushing the boundaries of their parents, caregivers, or educators.

It is the responsibility of an experienced child psychiatrist or developmental psychologist to determine whether a child's behaviour is age appropriate or extreme. To be diagnosed with ODD, a person must exhibit a recurring behavioural pattern for at least six months, which includes an angry or irritable mood, argumentative or defiant behaviour, and vindictiveness. At least one other person, including those outside the family, must be involved in the behaviour.

Temper tantrums are common in children under the age of three. These resemble some of the manifestations of oppositional defiant disorder, which is why the diagnosis process is frequently delayed. It is important to remember that these tantrums are age-appropriate and should not be misinterpreted as ODD.

In most cases, the condition is discovered after the child has completed pre-school or has just begun elementary school.

To make an accurate diagnosis, mental health professionals will conduct a thorough evaluation. They will consider the fact that the condition appears concurrently with other behavioural issues, attempting to distinguish between the associated manifestations.

What Is Involved in the Evaluation?

The assessment will consider the child's overall health, with special attention paid to symptoms suggestive of ODD (frequency, intensity, and timeframe). The specialist will inquire about the child's behaviour in various settings, such as at home, school, or when interacting with peers. A detailed history of the child's behaviour in different settings can aid in making an accurate diagnosis.

During the evaluation, family relationships will be examined because the family environment can contribute to the emergence of such issues.

The healthcare professional will take detailed notes on family situations and will discuss strategies used to manage the child's behaviour. They may also talk about less effective strategies and inquire about other mental health issues. Children with learning or communication disorders may require additional testing.

The specialist will want to speak with not only the child and his or her parents, but also with other caregivers and teachers when 'making the diagnosis. It is critical to investigate every aspect of the child's behaviour. Observing the child may be necessary, and assessment tools are frequently used to assess one's mental health.

If the psychiatrist suspects that the child has an underlying health condition, he or she may recommend further testing. Imaging studies and blood tests can both be used to identify underlying medical issues that may be contributing to the behavioural issue. The investigations can help to rule out potential causes such as drug abuse or mental health issues.

Direct interviews may be conducted depending on the child's age.

Children, on the other hand, are rarely capable of explaining why they behave the way they do, especially at a young age. They may also be unable to communicate with their parents or caregivers because they do not understand their symptoms. Long interviews with all adults involved in the child's upbringing should thus be conducted.

When Should a Diagnosis Be Obtained?

If the behavioural problems suggestive of ODD persist for more than six months, the child should be evaluated for ODD. If the child's behaviour is causing significant distress to other children and parents in the family, a diagnosis should be sought. The same is true when the child's educational performance suffers or their social relationships are hampered. If the child is unable to learn, has difficulty maintaining friendships, or is at risk of harm, ODD may be the cause.

Diagnostic Tests and Instruments

The Diagnostic and Statistical Manual of Mental Disorders (DSM-5) was developed and published by the American Psychiatric Association, and it provides precise diagnostic criteria for oppositional defiant disorder in children. The condition can range from mild to severe based on these criteria. The DSM checklist should always be compared to the child's behaviour, including direct responses from him/her (if old enough).

The Anxiety Disorder Interview Schedule is a structured interview in which both parents and children answer questions about mental health issues. The specialist may also use the Eyberg Child Behavior Inventory, which is completed by the parent and assesses the child's behaviour.

The Child Behavior Checklist, which is also filled out by the parent and contains specific sections that can be used for the assessment of suspected oppositional defiant disorder, is another potential tool for diagnosis. Finally, the Parental Stress Index can be used to determine how stressed a parent is based on the child's behaviour, other adults, and life events.

The sooner a diagnosis is made, the sooner an intervention plan can be developed and the child's behaviour can be improved. Parents who believe their children may have ODD should not put off seeing a specialist because only a trained professional can make an accurate diagnosis and recommend the most effective intervention strategies.

Chapter 2

Problematic behavior
Defiant behavior
Emotionally externalizing behavior
Aggressive behavior
Norm-breaking behavior
Provocative behavior
Hyperactive behavior

Age at onset of ODD
% of children with ODD diagnosis
25
20
15
10
5
0
0 1 2 3 4 5 6 7 8 9 10 11 12
Age (years)
Boys
Girls

Age at onset of CD
% of children with CD diagnosis
30
25
20
15
10
5
0
0 1 2 3 4 5 6 7 8 9 10 11 12
Age (years)
Boys
Girls

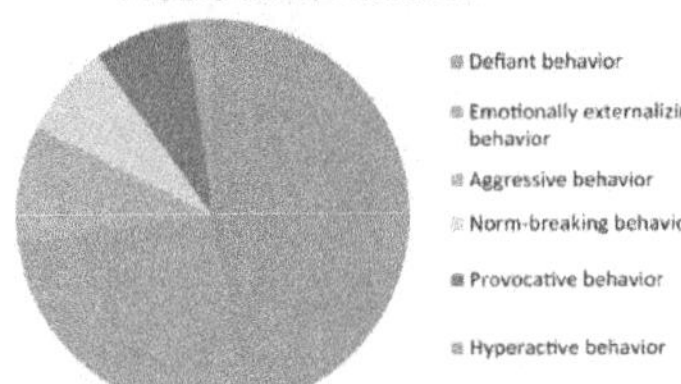

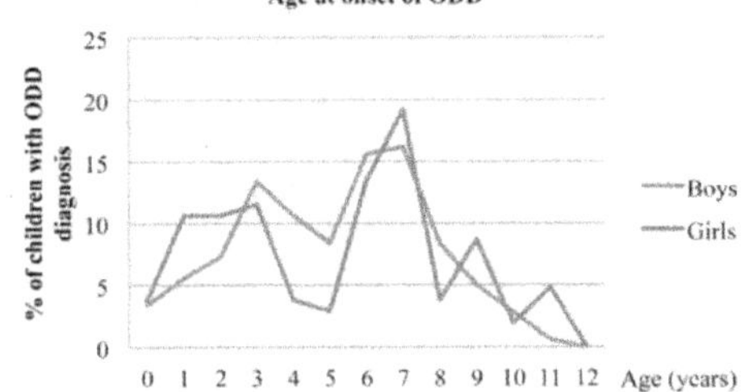

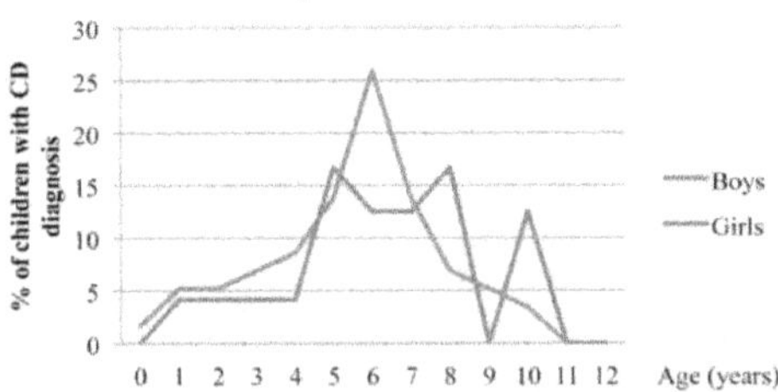

Chapter 3
A Parent's Guide for Children with ODD

There are many things you can do to help if your child has ODD and you are having difficulty dealing with them. When your child misbehaves, it is critical that you discuss their behaviour with them. Use a tone of voice that expresses empathy for their actions, and use language that allows for honest expression without blame. Explain the distinction between acceptable and unacceptable behaviour to ensure that they understand what is expected of them. Do not punish or shame them for past behaviours because this will only exacerbate the problem, but do provide a consequence if it occurs again in the future. If you become frustrated, ask yourself what is going on in your life that has triggered the behaviour, and then go do something to distract yourself from the situation. Try not to turn off your cell phone when you get home so you can get away from the situation.

DO: Discuss your feelings and the feelings of others. Explain that if he is upset about something, he can express his feelings to us. It's fine if he sobs; just don't yell at him or punish him. This is how we know we're talking to each other and not arguing about who was hurt the most by something.

Assure him that we are available to listen to him and assist him when he is in need. Tell him you love him and that he is unique.

Forget about your own emotions and stay in the moment, knowing that everything will be fine. It is acceptable for us to be angry or upset, but it is not acceptable for him to express this anger in front of our children. It may feel good when your child does this, but it is not acceptable in our house because we believe children should always do their best to behave respectfully and with good manners!

We will never tolerate inappropriate behaviour in our house. It is acceptable to be hurt, but it is not acceptable to cause harm to others.

If you are upset with your child because of his behaviour, express your displeasure to him. Do not express your displeasure because he does not act like his brother or sister, or because he is always so quiet. Make it clear to your children that we love them all equally and do not treat them differently because we are upset about their behaviour. If a parent says this in a heated moment, children may be confused about their family relationships and may take this confusion out on each other later.

It is not your fault if you feel powerless to control your child's behaviour. It's because he doesn't want to be respectful and calm. You can make your child's life extremely difficult by constantly reminding him of what he can and should not do. When children feel overly watched or controlled by their parents, they will vent their frustrations to one another. If not addressed immediately, this will cause resentment among siblings (and even children of other parents!) that could last well into adulthood.

Do not yell at your child if you are upset. If you get angry at him, he will learn that there is something wrong with him. Shouting is disrespectful to those around you and is never an appropriate way to treat a child. When they hear their name called or see your angry expression, they may believe that yelling is the only way to get things done.

Children may not understand that you're upset about something else if you're constantly upset and yelling at them. They may believe you are unwilling to discuss their behaviour. When they hear you yell and fight, they may become frustrated and take it out on their siblings. This can have a domino effect, with children failing to learn proper behaviour because no one sets a good example for them.

If you have a bad day, it does not mean that your child will begin acting out at home or at school. We cannot allow our bad days to affect how we treat our children. When a parent has a bad day at work and takes it out on their child at home, the child may have behavioural issues at school. This is not how you should treat your children.

Allow your child to be alone in his room while you take a time-out. Let him know you'll be back when you're feeling better so he knows it's not forever. He must understand that time-outs are only used when someone is upset and needs to get away from the situation. Do not respond when your child yells at you. If you do, he will learn that he can elicit a reaction from you when he is upset. This will cause other problems in your home because your children will understand how to irritate you with that behaviour. When your child understands that his actions affect your emotions, it can be difficult to correct him without becoming angry again.

If you lose your temper and become rude or cold to them, try not to respond to their behaviour with anger. That will only aggravate the situation for everyone and may lead to resentment between family members for years to come. Be consistent, fair, and predictable rather than yelling or humiliating them. If a parent imposes a punishment but then backs down in anger and forgives their child, the child will learn that he can get away with bad behaviour. Make it clear to your children that you will follow through on consequences because this is the only way they will learn how to behave appropriately in various situations.

If you set boundaries for your child, explain why they are there so he knows where his limits are and who is responsible for enforcing them.

If you set a boundary and your child disregards it, make it clear that he disobeyed the rule by not listening to you and that this is what will happen if he continues to disregard these rules.

Be mindful of your own emotions and how they may influence your child's behaviour. We can't control what our children do or how their actions affect us, but we can control how we respond to them. If you become angry with them and yell at them, they will not understand that you are truly upset about something else (such as their behaviour) and will believe that they are winning because you are upset. It's the same as being cold and ignoring them. They will believe you are upset with them for no reason and may act out as a result.

Take the time to recognise when your child is being challenged at home so you don't take it out on him with your own behaviour. If you become frustrated with him, you must learn to direct your rage away from him before it consumes you! Anger and frustration directed at children can create feelings of hopelessness and helplessness in them, exacerbating their problems.

If your child is acting out or displaying negative behaviours or discipline techniques, it is critical to investigate what is causing these behaviours. Your child may be attempting to manipulate you because he refuses to do things the way you want him to or follow the rules you have established for him. He may be well aware that these behaviours are unacceptable and that he will irritate you if he continues. The more negative reactions you exhibit, the more likely it is that your child will continue this behaviour in the hopes of getting a different reaction from you. This is when children will test limits and boundaries at home because they will believe they are getting away with something by having their parents behave in this manner.

Tell your child how much he respects, loves, and trusts your family and what kinds of behaviour make his family happy. Teach them to respect and appreciate their family by respecting themselves, others, and the environment.

When they are not listening and still acting out, use a time-out. If you have to tell him he's acting out, he'll realize it's a serious situation. If he continues to misbehave, take him to a room where he can be alone or with the child who has requested a time-out.

This will teach him that if he refuses to listen and obey you, there will be consequences. Having just one parent argues with another sends a negative message that parents are not in control of themselves or their children's behaviour.

If you feel like you're losing control of your children, talk to your spouse and/or any other adults in the family about getting things in order before you lose it and start yelling at them. The more you yell at them, the worse their behaviour will be around you. If your family is having discipline issues, talk to other parents about their experiences so that you can learn from them as well.

Be mindful of how others treat your children when they misbehave. It will not have the same effect on your children if others treat their behaviour with respect and kindness.

Set some boundaries for your child so that he understands what will happen if he does not abide by them. You don't want to teach him that he can make you angry simply by acting up, but you do want him to understand that there are consequences when he doesn't behave properly at home. When you set and stick to a limit, explain why this is happening and what behaviour you expect him to exhibit rather than what you don't. This will teach him how to understand limits in his life while also demonstrating to him that there is a way to behave properly without being punished.

For good behaviour, use positive reinforcement. Make a point of rewarding your child for good behaviour or times when he isn't acting out or misbehaving. This will help him realize that being a good person and doing the right thing is far preferable to not getting what he wants (or doesn't want). He'll also try to act out in order to get your attention, but if you give him positive attention without making him act out, he won't feel the need to draw your attention with bad behaviour.

If your child is having difficulty managing his emotions or is depressed, seek medical attention. This could be a sign of something more serious, in which case your child's doctor will need to prescribe medication.

If your child is acting out because he does not want to be in a particular situation, he will make it difficult for you to have him where you do not want him. He'll act out and refuse to go where you want him to, so consider how much trouble you'll be in if this continues or how tired you'll be when he does this. If your situation is that bad, perhaps there are other ways for your family to get things done so that you can spend time together at the park or somewhere else fun.

Consider times when you have acted out and how your parents reacted to your actions. Were they mad at you? Did it help you learn how to behave, or did it make you want to act out more in the hope of getting a different result? If your parents' behaviour was ineffective, don't repeat it! Consider what was considered respectful behaviour at the time and try to apply it so that your child understands how he should behave.

Make sure you're ready to deal with bad behaviour if it becomes a problem. Because there is some unpredictability, make sure you have all of the important information on hand in case something goes wrong.

Children will continue to be children. If you have never dealt with a situation like this before, you may end up simply reacting to their bad behaviour, which they may learn how to get out of by repeating it enough times to receive a reward. Remember that you want to teach them how to behave appropriately, not how to use your reaction against you to get what they want. If this is a problem between you and your child, find a way for him to understand what kind of behaviour is acceptable and don't let him act out to get your attention if he doesn't like something.

Children can be very stubborn at times, but if you keep a sense of humor and demonstrate that you are not upset with them, they may respond to your behaviour rather than their own reaction to the situation. Just make sure you don't pay too much attention to them when they misbehave, or they won't learn how to behave properly.

If you have a problem in your family that is affecting your children's behaviour, talk to other parents about what you can do so that you know what type of behaviour will work for your family. When their children are misbehaving in their homes, they should not use each other as free babysitters. The issue must be addressed and resolved as soon as possible.

If your family continues to have issues with misbehaving children, make a plan of action for dealing with the behaviour. This will prepare you for what to do if something similar happens, preventing you from panicking and acting out against your children.

It is critical that your children understand how they are expected to behave at home and outside of it so that they know what is expected of them before getting into an argument or situation with other people, or before getting into trouble at school or other places where there may be consequences for their actions.

Chapter 4
Happy children are raised by peaceful parents.

Parenting entails a great deal of responsibility. It is a full-time job for the rest of one's life that no parent should ignore or undervalue.

It is common for parents to be unable to fulfill their responsibilities for a variety of reasons. After all, they are human, and they may be mentally distressed and neglect their responsibilities. This is completely natural, but a child will not comprehend the situation. If a parent acts in this manner, the child and their upbringing will suffer greatly.

In such cases, the child may develop a mental illness as an adult and be unable to live life to the fullest. Their personality may become severely distorted, causing the child to become depressed, stressed out, and dissatisfied. That is why it is critical that parents understand their role in preventing this from happening to their children.

As a parent, you should strive to maintain a calm and peaceful demeanor while raising your children. In this section of the book, I'll discuss some of the tools that will assist you as a parent in dealing with your child's aggressive behavior while maintaining your inner peace.

Improved comprehension

One of the most important reasons for taking a calm approach to raising your child is the development of a deeper understanding between you and your child. One of the most difficult issues that both parents and children face is a lack of understanding for one another. The main thing to try to overcome is the obvious generation gap between you. A parent may not immediately comprehend how the new generations, of which their child is a member, think and act. A parent may try to limit perfectly normal behavior for their child, or they may be unable to understand what their child is saying.

Similarly, a child of a new generation will most likely never understand their parents' mentality, standards, and molarity.

Children will have difficulty understanding where their parents are coming from because they belong to older generations and thus have a more "old-school" approach to life.

If parents become impatient and try to impose their beliefs on their children in this situation, the child is likely to rebel and refuse to follow their parents' guidance.

That is why it is critical to maintaining your cool when dealing with your child. If you raise your children in a peaceful environment, they will be more receptive to your point of view, and you will be able to better understand your child.

Increase Trust in Your Relationship

Another significant advantage of a calm approach to parenting is the trust that will develop between you and your child. One of the most important aspects of any relationship is trust. Consider it this way. Would you blindly follow someone you don't completely trust?

The same is true for children. As a parent, you are your child's first role model and source of rules and standards for coping with the world.

If your child sees you constantly angry and stressed out, yelling at them and losing your temper in front of them, he or she will not be able to develop trust in you. They would rather stay away and not share their thoughts and feelings with you than speak up confidently.

In this case, a calm demeanor is extremely beneficial. If you create a safe space for your child to communicate their problems with you and take the time to actually listen to what they have to say, they will naturally come to trust you. They will understand that no matter what they are going through, you will listen and understand. The most important aspect of a parent-child relationship is probably trust.

Problem Solving Made Simple

Another advantage of peaceful parenting is that you will be able to solve problems more easily. When we are upset, stressed out, or angry, it is impossible to solve any problem satisfactorily. Consider what would happen if your child came to you for help while you are in that state of emotional turmoil. Would you be able to provide the best assistance possible? The answer is most likely no. If you force yourself into problem-solving mode while you're upset, you're much more likely to aggravate the situation for everyone involved, including yourself and your child. This, in turn, will have an impact on your entire family dynamic.

On the other hand, if you strive for a peaceful and calm state of mind, you will find it easier to deal with problems. Your mind will be at peak performance, and your solutions to any adversity will be far more effective.

Keep Special Moments in Mind

Another advantage of having a peaceful mind is that you will be able to truly cherish all of those special moments with your child. When we are in constant emotional turmoil, we often miss the special moments that make our lives meaningful. This also applies to all of the wonderful moments you may have with your child. Consider this: your child comes to you with exciting news about something that happened at school or with their friends, but you're having a bad day and don't want a noisy child, so you tell them to go to their room and leave you alone for a while. You will have missed out on a crucial stage in your child's development and growth, as well as the opportunity to share their triumphs with them. This will also cause serious harm to your child.

Obtain Respect

If your child sees you always trying to solve problems with a level head and a peaceful attitude, this will increase the amount of respect your child has for you as an adult in their lives. If, on the other hand, you let your emotions get the best of you and consistently exhibit aggressive behavior around your children, they will eventually want to avoid the toxic environment of their home as much as possible.

While we are far from perfect, it is critical that our children do not perceive us as disrespectful and angry adults. Rather, parents should strive to be role models that their children admire and want to emulate when faced with stressful situations. If your child observes you remaining calm under duress, confronting problems head-on and rationally, and, most importantly, still showing love and affection for your family, they will emulate you as adults.

How Do You Get Your Child to Stop Yelling?

People who express their rage by yelling will occasionally lash out at a child who has inadvertently enraged them.

Yelling at someone is never helpful in resolving a problem, but yelling at a child is even more problematic. Assume that a person three times your height, someone who is supposed to be looking out for you, is suddenly yelling at you for doing something you didn't even realize was wrong. This can be extremely dangerous for your child. It is hurtful and will almost certainly lead to them becoming people who yell at others to express their frustrations.

If you are the type of person who yells when angry, here are some more ways to control your anger before you start screaming at your child.

Understand Your Triggers

The desire to yell at someone rarely, if ever, appears out of nowhere. In all likelihood, your rage has been building for a period of time — shorter for some than longer for others — and then something happens to set it off.

If you have an ODD child, your child is most likely a recurring trigger for your anger, and you will end up yelling at them before you realize it.

That is why understanding your triggers is critical. Consider a time when you lost your temper and yelled at your child.

Examine the events that led up to the yelling and try to determine what triggered it. If you make this a habit, you will eventually be able to identify your triggers as they occur and prevent yourself from yelling at your child. Those triggers will lose their power over you over time and patience, and you will no longer be upset to the point of yelling.

Give Children a Heads-Up

This works well if you already know what your triggers are. It's a good idea to warn your child about the kinds of behaviors that make you angry. If you want to change their behavior, telling them that it makes you angry can help them change their behavior, preventing you from yelling at them.

If you're already frustrated and on the verge of yelling, express your frustration to your child. If they're doing something that you don't want to change in the long run, but rather just now, tell them that what they're doing is making you uncomfortable or upset, and ask them to stop for a while.

Create a Yes List

A Yes List is a list of things you will agree to do before yelling at someone. Take a pen and paper and make a list of everything on this list. It could be anything from going to the bathroom and taking some deep breaths to jog in place or anything else that gets you away from the situation. Put that list somewhere visible, like the fridge or a mirror, so you can refer to it whenever you feel like yelling. If you notice your temper rising, try one or more of the items on the list.

Later, teach the lesson

Under normal circumstances, the best time to teach your child a lesson is immediately after they have done something wrong. If you have a quick temper, it's best to wait until you've calmed down before imparting wisdom. If you lose your cool and yell at your child after they make a mistake, you're unlikely to be thinking about teaching them anything. You're probably just venting your rage and blaming your child.

In this case, you should use the previous techniques for defusing your anger and getting your child to stop doing what is making you angry. Once you've calmed down, you'll be able to communicate what bothered you about their behavior and they'll understand what you're trying to teach them.

Respecting Your Child's Individuality

In many ways, new generations outperform their forefathers. Today's children are speeding up the evolution of humanity as a whole. If adults took the time to listen to what they had to say and carefully answer their questions, we could see the knowledge accumulated over many generations in their comments.

Children from newer generations, in particular, exhibit more emotional responses than children from previous generations. Our parents (and their parents) would never have dared to question an authority figure at home or at school, as children do today. Emotions must be expressed rather than bottled up in order for a child to grow into a balanced and happy adult. Allowing our children to do this and learning from them is the best way for our society to progress.

Overcoming years (and generations) of repressed emotions is not easy. But if we look at our children, listen to what they have to say, and especially try to identify what we find most annoying about their attitude, we will learn something about ourselves.

If you believe your child is not treating you with respect, consider whether you are treating your child with the same respect you expect to be shown. Many times, a particular behavior or attitude that irritates us about someone else, particularly our children, is simply a reflection of something we dislike about ourselves.

Another instance is when a parent attempts to impose their way of life on their children. A child or adolescent may already have a preferred method of doing something, but a parent insists on it because "that's how things are done" or "because I said so." This will cause an ODD child or a rebellious teenager to tell you to back off and mind your own business. Children and teenagers have the right to make their own decisions, and if what they are doing is not causing them or anyone else harm, take a step back and let them do their thing. It is critical that you remember that a child is not yours to control, but rather that you try to see the world through their eyes and experiences.

"Should I simply give in and let my kids do whatever they want?" I understand your query. Both yes and no. Yes, if what they want to do does not harm them or others, or is not illegal. Allow your child to be themselves, to be whom they want to be, and to express themselves freely. Parents may not always agree with a particular aspect of their child's personality, but they must respect it nonetheless.

Assume Lily is a rambunctious adolescent. She has a bad habit of leaving her belongings all over the floor. Rather than becoming enraged and demanding that she clean up after herself, you could try asking her why she prefers to leave her belongings strewn about rather than pick them up. Is she more at ease and safe in a cluttered room than in a clean one? If the answer is a genuine "yes," you can tell her that you are the polar opposite — that you do not feel at ease in such an environment. Then you can try to reach an agreement. You can tell her that she can keep her room however she wants as long as she keeps the common areas of the house tidy.

This will promote peace between you because you will no longer be irritated by the mess in her room, and she will make an effort to be tidy in other areas of the house.

When you open yourself up to the idea of learning about your child's personality and trying to accept the aspects of it that you don't particularly like, your relationship with your child is bound to change. Don't be afraid to share your thoughts with your child! They will reciprocate if they see you making an effort to meet them halfway.

They will mature into individuals who are secure in their life choices and understand that they are free to be themselves.

If you notice that your child has little or no interest in exploring the world, cannot find a hobby and has no desire to be independent or autonomous, you should intervene as a parent to offer assistance. The first step is to strengthen your relationship with your child by showing them affection without them having to ask or fight for it. Allow them to feel at ease in their relationship with you.

Here are some suggestions to assist your child in discovering their hidden potential.

Tip No. 1 — Show Your Child Love

Hug your child and reassure him or her that you love them and will always take care of them. This is especially important before sending your child to school or to an unfamiliar location.

Encourage your child's ideas, thoughts, and passions. "It's incredible that you did this all by yourself!" is preferable to "I like what you did!"

Tip No. 2 — Allow Your Child to Self-Teach

Allow your child to try to grasp the essence of things on their own. Make no attempt to force them into early development. A child who has experienced the incredible feeling of discovering something on their own will later develop a self-sufficient personality.

Unfortunately, most of today's children do not have the luxury of experiencing the thrill of a new discovery; the Internet already provides all of the answers before they even know what questions to ask.

Make an effort to provide opportunities for your child to learn something new on their own, away from external influences or expectations.

Tip No. 3 — Allow Your Child Free Play Time

As previously stated, your child requires time away from school, homework, and organized recreational activities for free play. You have shown your child affection and created an environment in which they can learn new things. Now is the time to sit back and watch as your child does their own thing. How much time do they devote to a particular activity? How long do they think and plan before drawing, stacking blocks, dancing, and so on?

If your child becomes bored too quickly, resist the urge to play with them right away. Some parents will go to great lengths to keep their children entertained at all times. If you've already spent time playing with your child and feel the need to take a step back, allow them to entertain themselves. "I'll be right here, I'm not going anywhere, but I can't play with you right now," try telling them.

Tip #4 — Give your child authority and responsibilities.

If you allow your child to drive and make their own decisions, they will gradually learn that they have control over their lives and will strive to reach their full potential. Provide your child with an environment in which they can freely express themselves. Allow your child as much freedom as possible. Rather than picking out clothes for them, ask them what they want to wear. Allow them to choose what they want for breakfast or when they want to go to bed.

Trust that your child will make the right decisions for themselves and give them some responsibility — for example, ask them to make lunch for the family or assign them some housework.

Your role as a parent is to decide how much freedom to give your child and in what areas of their lives to relinquish some or all of your control. It is up to you to determine when your child is ready to be in charge of more responsibilities.

Chapter 5
Control Their Reluctant Behavior

Growing teenagers find it difficult to communicate openly with their parents.

To avoid problems caused by the aforementioned generation gaps, you must establish an open line of communication as a parent. Maintaining open and honest communication also prevents your child from developing aggressive behavior.

The bond between a parent and their child is unique. Children rely entirely on their parents for care, security, and love when they are young. They naturally regard their parents as their closest companions, protectors, and confidantes. They rely on their parents to love and support them unconditionally, regardless of their flaws and mistakes.

When your child reaches the age of adolescence, he or she may begin to exhibit aggressive behaviors. Their emotions become more complex, and they find themselves suddenly lacking the words to communicate their thoughts and needs to their parents. This can result in misunderstandings and fights between you and your child.

Teenagers want to become adults as soon as possible! This can be stressful for them because they are still developing their self-identity and learning how to interact with the outside world. These are trying times for your child; despite their best efforts, they feel lost and vulnerable.

It is normal for a teenager's mind to become cluttered with confusion, conflict, doubts, anxiety, and other negative emotions.

As your child goes through this difficult period in their life, it is your responsibility as a parent to open lines of communication with them. Assist them in putting their thoughts and feelings into words, provide a safe space for them to do so, and assure them that what they are experiencing is normal. Your teen will remain closed off unless you create the right environment at home for them to express themselves, and you will become a mere spectator in these trying times.

Reduce your expectations to make parenting a teenager a little bit easier. Accept your teen's interests (even if you don't fully understand them). Allow you're teen to do their own thing rather than trying to manage them. Try parenting classes and find activities that both you and your teen will enjoy.

Adopting Highly Effective Parenting Paradigms

If you want your child to grow up with a positive attitude, you must first adopt the paradigms of highly effective parents, which are as follows:

The worldview of children differs from that of their parents.

As a parent, the first step is to change your mind about your world model. You must first understand and accept that your worldview is not the same as that of your child or teen. You should not attempt to impose your opinions on them. What appears to you as wise, worldly advice may appear to your teen as nagging, and they may perceive you as attempting to control them?

Parenting a teenager necessitates a great deal of comprehension, tolerance, humility, and patience. In some ways, this is likely to be the most difficult time for a parent. Even so, parenting a teen does not have to be a nightmare. Here are some techniques you can use to make parenting your adolescent easier and more enjoyable.

Technique 1: How to Create a Child-Raising Method

Some parents appear to be extremely successful in raising their children to be responsible, caring, and honest adults, whereas many others simply do not seem to get it right. To begin, it is critical to recognize that it is your responsibility as a parent to assist your children in developing a good, strong moral character. This does not happen by accident; it requires a significant amount of effort, time, and focus.

There are several parenting tips that will be very useful and valuable in helping your teen develop a strong character that will help them in the future. However, if you have a parenting partner, it won't matter how effective these techniques are if you don't work together as a team.

You should always be in your partner's corner, and they should always be in yours. This necessitates communication and regular discussions about the values you want to instill in your children, as well as the best way to do so. When it comes to discipline, love, and upbringing, collaboration and constant communication will keep you and your partner on the same page.

When the going gets tough, as it inevitably will, having a few extra ideas on hand can make life a whole lot easier — for both kids and parents. This also necessitates the full commitment of the parenting figures in the child's life. Here are a few more ideas that have helped many parents.

Tip #1: Teach, Discuss, and Demonstrate Beneficial Qualities

As a parent, you must be a firm believer in discussing with your child what is and isn't appropriate behavior. However, simply discussing it is insufficient. As the saying goes, if you talk the talk, you must walk the walk.

So, while it is important to teach your child the value of patience, for example, by explaining why we have to wait our turn at the grocery store or to ride a ride at an amusement park, it is equally important for you not to lose your cool when you are in a hurry and are forced to wait as well.

Tip #2: Teach Your Child Responsibility

Chores are essential for teaching your child the valuable lesson of responsibility. Giving your child tasks on a regular basis is an excellent way to instill self-reliance and encourage pride in a job well done.

When your child has completed their task, give them a hug, a thumbs up, or a pat on the back to show your appreciation. Always remember to express your gratitude for the work they've done and how much they've helped you.

Tip #3: Be Specific in Your Praise!

Praise your children when they exhibit positive character traits. This is a great way to reinforce the traits you want them to develop.

For example, if you want to help your child learn how to be a good friend and value strong friendships, making a habit of giving them specific praise is a great place to start.

It's natural to want to do more of the things that get us compliments. When your child understands or does something kind or polite, make a point of telling them what you think.

Honesty is another desirable trait that can be cultivated with the right wording. When your child is truthful about something they've done or haven't done, praise them without reprimanding them, such as "I like how you were truthful about not finishing your schoolwork." Let's get together and see what else needs to be done so you can get started as soon as possible.

Tip #4: Be the best role model you can be.

Of course, modeling positive character traits in your own behavior is the most effective way to help your child develop positive character traits. After all, you are your child's most important role model.

You must decide and vow to be the best example of the qualities you most value and want to instill in your child. If you make a habit of doing them, your child will undoubtedly notice — perhaps not consciously at first, but rest assured that your actions will have a positive effect on a deeper level.

Remember that you're doing more than just raising a well-behaved child when you follow this parenting advice. You're bringing up a child who is responsible, kind and has a strong sense of right and wrong.

It is not always easy to help your child develop a strong moral character, but it is extremely rewarding. After all, these values and talents will benefit your child for the rest of his or her life!

Technique 2: Improving Your Understanding of Your Child

You will most likely learn what to expect from your child after some time. However, knowing what to expect from your teen is not enough; you must also take it into consideration.

Technique 2: Improving Your Understanding of Your Child

You will most likely learn what to expect from your child after some time. But knowing what to expect from your teen isn't enough; you need to go one step further and reach out into their world. This requires you to understand them, their language, their points of view, and the problems they face on a daily basis, as well as know what they expect from you as a parent.

What are the Top Five Expectations of Teens from Parents?

- Being accepted and loved; 2. Being recognized and validated
- Liberty and Independence
- Being Reliable
- Having Respect

Understanding your adolescent can be a difficult task at times. Most of the time, your conversations may devolve into name-calling, loud arguments, and miscommunication. Rather than being unhappy, which only serves to perpetuate the pattern, concentrate on figuring out what makes your child tick. It will be easier to understand them and develop a long-lasting and productive relationship with them once you learn to communicate with them and acknowledge their feelings.

Tip #1: Keep an Open Line of Communication with Your Teen

You should reconsider how you communicate with your adolescent. Is your communication dominated by orders, complaints, and punishment? Do you have open communication where they can freely express their thoughts and feelings? You will be unable to understand your child unless you encourage them to speak.

You should initiate the conversation by asking an open-ended question. Ask your child or teen about their school day, and keep asking open-ended questions to encourage them to talk. If they aren't in the mood, simply let them know you are available to listen to them when they are.

Use the time you spend together, such as in the car or setting the table for dinner, to initiate communication with them. Pay attention to what they're saying and express genuine interest in their interests and hobbies. The main goal of this approach is to simply understand what motivates and makes your child happy. It is about learning about their goals and inspirations.

Tip #2: Respect Your Child's Emotions

It is critical that your child understands that their feelings are important to you as a parent. They may become angry, frustrated, or embarrassed at times. Instead of dismissing them and telling them to calm down, provide them with the assistance they require.

When you're having a heated debate, it's best to let your child speak. It's critical that you pay attention to them, nod, and \ maintain eye contact with them. If possible, repeat what they said to demonstrate that you are paying attention and acknowledging their feelings. A hug is a magical and powerful thing that you might find useful at times as well.

Tip #3: Value Your Child's Desire for Independence.

Every time your teen challenges your authority, remember that they are simply attempting to demonstrate their independence. You must remember that your child is developing both physically and mentally. This is the beginning of their independence for them.

As previously stated, this requires you to be flexible and give up some control. For example, it's a good idea to let them pick their own clothes — both when shopping for new ones and when deciding what to wear for the day.

Respecting your child's privacy is another aspect of independence. If you haven't already, consider knocking before entering their room, asking for permission to enter, and giving them some alone time.

Keep an eye on your child if he or she appears to be spending too much time alone. If your child appears withdrawn, talk to them and ask if they have a problem they'd like to discuss.

Tip #4: Understand How a Teen's Brain Works

As a parent, you must understand that a teenager's brain is constantly changing. You are more likely to understand and accommodate their behaviors if you recognize and appreciate this fact.

Your teen's reactions may appear irrational to you because different parts of the brain mature at different rates.

In reality, the part of the brain associated with reward, motivation, and impulsiveness matures much earlier than the part associated with the task of weighing the pros and cons of any given action.

As a result, your adolescent does not share her perspective on the consequences of their actions. With this in mind, it will be beneficial to discuss the risks associated with risky decisions with your child.

Technique 3: Educating and Guiding Your Child to Make Sound Decisions

The culture of a community is its way of life. It refers to the socially transmitted habits, traditions, customs, and beliefs of a group of people at any given time.

Teenagers are frequently left behind in terms of catching up with norms, values, behavior patterns, practices, etiquette, social groups, religion, superstitions, and spirituality, among other cultural concepts. There are several guides that can help you guide your teen down the cultural path you believe is best for them, but keep in mind that they will ultimately make this decision for themselves.

Keep an eye on your teen's behavior, academic performance, and relationships with peers, friends, teachers, and others in their inner circle. This, along with an open line of communication, should help you understand what issues your teen may be having with the world around them.

If their behavior appears to be out of the ordinary in a way that is negatively affecting them, go back to basics and try to re-establish communication with them. Find ways to get your teen to open up to you and talk to you about their concerns. Getting a teen to open up is difficult, but with the right techniques (being friendly, listening to them without judgment, offering support, etc.), it is certainly a goal that can be achieved.

After your child has opened up to you and told you about their problems, it's time to offer some advice. Express to them which option you believe is best for them, but always take the time to explain why you believe that option is best for them.

The Best Decisions

Your teen must understand that their decisions must always be in accordance with local laws and regulations. Any illegal activities must be clearly explained to them, as well as the consequences of participating in them.

Situations you may encounter include:
Situation #1: When Your Child Hasn't Made a Choice

If your child or teen is unsure what to do in a given situation, the one thing you must not do is try to impose your views on them. Make time for both of you to analyze your child's problem and outline what you believe is the best solution or course of action to take.

Consider comparing various solutions to a problem and attempting to explain the consequences or benefits that each of those solutions may have. The most important thing is that you do not force your child to make a decision; instead, allow them to consider each potential solution, analyze the outcome, and ultimately make their own decision.

Situation No. 2: When Your Child Has Made a Decision

In some cases, your teen may have already decided how to solve a problem, and all that remains is for them to carry out their decision. In that case, it is your responsibility as a parent to show your love and support while also offering to assist them in carrying out their decision if necessary. This vote of confidence in your teen will make them feel trusted, and they will come to you with any future problems.

Technique 4: Assisting Your Child in Breaking down the Barriers That Separate Them from Their Families and Society

Teenagers frequently express feelings of being "alone in a room full of people." Your teen may begin to feel as if they don't belong anywhere, which can be very distressing at this age. Teens need to feel like they belong and fit in with their surroundings in order to feel secure and safe.

When your teen says, "I don't fit in," what they're really saying is, "I don't feel safe." They feel strange and alienated, which leads to anxiety. While this is most likely more common in schools, teens can have this feeling anywhere, including at home.

You can do a lot as a parent to change the family environment — everything this book has discussed so far will help with that — but you can't make society adapt to your child. No matter how much you want to change the world to accommodate them, the only thing you can do is work with your child to teach them the social skills they need to cope with their feelings of isolation.

First, make sure your child feels loved and supported at home.

Teenagers who feel rejected by their families are more likely to engage in defiant behavior. As a result, as a parent of an adolescent, you must pay closer attention to your child and concentrate on understanding their feelings and desires.

Another effective way to make your child feel included in the family is to plan activities in which everyone participates, such as weekly family meetings, parties, or picnics. It is critical that each member of the family participates fairly. This way, your teen will be exposed to the value of family unity while also receiving much-needed solidarity, fun, attention, and love from family.

Teach Your Child to Be a Good Friend (Skill #2)

Without a doubt, friendship is an important aspect of any child's development and growth. Sharing, compromising problem-solving, forgiving, and most other social skills are learned through play and misunderstandings with friends.

Teach your child empathy from a young age by participating in social events, making birthday cards for friends and family members, and lending a helping hand to those younger than them and the elderly.

The skills they learn at home will naturally transfer to the outside world.

3. Recognize Your Child's Friendship Style

Some children thrive in large groups of friends, whereas others prefer to interact with only one or two children at a time. It is critical that you understand what works best for your child and do not force them into uncomfortable social situations.

Remember that what works for you might not work for them. Allow your child to be happy playing with one friend and do not force them to attend a large birthday party if it upsets them.

Open Your Home to Your Child's Friendship

Make it clear to your child that your home is open to their friends.

When they're younger, you can organize playdates and activities for them.

As your child enters adolescence, they will want to plan their own activities with their friends, but this does not preclude them from visiting you. Let your teen know that their friends are welcome at any time, and provide them with privacy and a safe space to have fun.

Help Your Child Work through Family and Friendship Issues

Troubles

Miscommunication is common among family members, friends, and peers. Your teen may require assistance from time to time in processing the emotions that arise as a result of such conflicts. Because teenagers are notoriously private, they may not immediately inform you of a fight or misunderstanding with a friend. Keep an eye out for signs that your teen is upset and try to talk to them about it.

Your teen may even consider ending a friendship after a fight, depending on the severity of the conflict. It is not your responsibility to step in and solve their problems in this case. Rather, teach them the skills they will need to deal with such situations. Use your own experience to demonstrate to them that everyone has disagreements at times, but that it is important to listen to the other person's side of the argument and try to be understanding. Explain the importance of not making rash decisions during an argument, and that it is preferable to wait until they have calmed down before attempting to resolve the issue.

Encourage Your Child to Participate in Extracurricular Activities

Encourage a teen who is feeling isolated to participate in activities that they enjoy. This could include anything from sports clubs to music or art programs, both in and out of school. This way, your child will be able to connect with other kids his or her age who share similar interests.

Skill #7: Enlist the Help of Experts

If you suspect that your teen is experiencing feelings of isolation and alienation, don't be afraid to seek professional help. Severe feelings of isolation, if not addressed early, can lead to depression and low self-esteem.

Technique 5: Put Yourself in the Shoes of Your Child to Better Understand Them

During these trying years, your adolescent will be fighting multiple battles at the same time. The best thing you can do as their parent is to show them that you care by providing support and understanding. Put yourself in their shoes as much as possible. After all, we were all teenagers once and know exactly what it's like to be in that situation. Remember what you wanted, thought, and felt as a teenager, and keep that perspective close to your heart when assisting your teen.

Keep in mind that teenagers require assistance in learning how to manage their emotions. Don't lose your cool when your teen has an emotional outburst.

Rather, try to maintain you're cool to make it easier to resolve the conflict.

Your adolescent requires space to develop their personality.

After a certain age, your adolescent will begin to develop at a rapid pace. All of the visible physical changes are only the tip of the iceberg; the majority of their developmental changes are psychological in nature.

Offer Assistance

Allow your teen to develop their own personality and go through their own process of self-discovery. On several occasions, your teen's emotions will overpower their better judgment. Allow them to express their dissatisfaction until they calm down. However, you must set boundaries — for example, if you do not tolerate name-calling, this can be a good place to draw the line of what is acceptable during their outbursts.

Being a teenager is difficult. This is a time when your child requires a lot of your help. It is normal to have a love-hate relationship with teenagers at times, but by offering your love and support, you will be on the right track to assisting them in getting through these difficult years.

Chapter 6
A Healthy Way of Life for People with ODD

Children and Adolescents

Mental and physical health are inextricably linked, and both should be prioritized.

Never underestimate the importance of leading a healthy lifestyle. Can, however,

Dietary restrictions assist children with behavioral issues such as ODD.

Is this a myth, or is it true? Given how many other disorders exist, are those that are associated with ODD and can co-occur, teaching?

It is not a bad idea to encourage your child to live a healthy lifestyle.

There are also specific nutrients that can be targeted to improve health.

The ability of the brain to function and your child's overall mood worthy of mention And why not include some healthy exercise?

In their interests and activities? This chapter discusses how to best nutrition and physical health approach for your ODD child and

It will also provide some great family-time ideas for a teen with a happy ending in mind

Are There Any Dietary Requirements?

Although a medical professional will almost certainly refer you to claims a therapist or, in a more serious case, prescribe medication

The idea of taking specific nutrients in the form of supplements has emerged in debates and articles, the authors of these articles claim that the

If your child is deficient in certain nutrients, it is worthwhile to try them suffering from severe ODD symptoms Nutrients are found in food.

They are also available as supplements. The conversation

The sections that follow will go over when and how to use supplements.

You can look for nutrient-rich foods that are high in the good stuff in the most natural way possible

Fatty Acids Omega 3

Omega 3 is an all-around miracle worker, and ADHD patients benefit greatly from it.

Known to consume a concentrated form of Omega 3 to aid in their symptoms. This is due to the fact that the body cannot produce this fatty acid create itself, is an important nutrient for maintenance and, in the case of

The development of the brain in children Omega 3 fatty acids do not cause

It not only helps with ADHD, but it also has a slew of other advantages.

Ailments affecting brain function affect both young and old people. It is also regarded as an essential nutrient for humans but is not widely available in a variety of foods. This is why a lot of people choose to take an Omega 3 supplement to compensate for its lack of our modern way of eating Omega 3 contains two kinds of fatty acids known as

EPA and DHA are essential for optimal brain function development beginning in childhood, but EPA is especially beneficial when

When it comes to mental health problems. To use Omega 3 for therapeutic purposes

Look for measures such as treating ADHD or ODD symptoms.

Fish oil or supplement with a higher EPA to DHA ratio.

The suggested ratio is at least twice as much EPA as DHA.

One of the problems Omega 3 fatty acids have been studied to help with is and reduce anxiety. A study conducted at the China Medical University

University Hospital, where subjects were compared based on whether they were provided either Omega 3 polyunsaturated fats or placebos

Patients who were given Omega 3 fatty acids had a surprising outcome showed significant reductions in their anxiety levels Anxiety is a mental illness.

a component found not only in ODD but in the majority of its co-occurring conditions Aside from that, keep in mind that your child's

The brain will develop throughout childhood and adolescence.

Apart from that, omega-3 fatty acids are essential for neural development.

It appears that having these advantages for children and teenagers with ODD is beneficial.

It's almost odd that there isn't a community van driving around in

"Remember to give your children their daily vitamins," the streets yelled a healthy dose of Omega 3 fatty acids" over a crackling megaphone

(Demko, 2018).

What Would We Do If We Didn't Have Omega 3?

Don't Forget to Include Vitamin E!

This is correct. Vitamin E is essential because it aids in the absorption of nutrients.

Omega 3! That is the primary reason. However, because we're

Let's take a look and see if Vitamin E has any other advantages.

Vitamin E appears to have numerous advantages and functions which include better vision, healthier blood, healthier skin, and brain health Vitamin E is also a good source of antioxidants safeguard human cells from free radical damage the positive

The good news about Vitamin E is that it is not as scarce in our daily diet as are Omega 3 fatty acids. You can obtain Vitamin E by consuming peanuts, olive oil, canola oil, almonds, or even meat and dairy products made from milk So, while Vitamin E aids in the acquisition of the best

It has its own advantages apart from your supercharged Omega 3. And,

If you give a child a supplement, it is not necessary to provide one.

On a regular basis, they get a good old peanut butter sandwich (Mayo).

2020 Clinic Staff).

Zinc

Zinc has an intriguing benefit. While the research was being carried out.

Researchers discovered that children with ADHD had lower levels of zinc than children without ADHD, and it was hypothesized that

There could be a connection. We now know that zinc can have a It can have a therapeutic effect on children and teenagers with ODD decrease impulsivity and hyperactivity, but, strangely, not in any way related to inattention it is also worth noting

Zinc, like Omega 3 fatty acids, is considered an essential nutrient acids, implying that the human body does not produce nutrients. If your child or adolescent with ODD exhibits any of these two symptoms,

You can visit your doctor and request a check for symptoms that are not only common in ODD but also in co-occurring conditions is carried out on your child's zinc levels. This could solve a problem.

You previously did not know how to solve the problem, and this did not produce results solely through therapy Zinc levels that are too low can be dangerous.

Too high levels, on the other hand, can be harmful. So, if you're thinking about giving,

If you want to give your child a supplement, you should first consult with a doctor.

Magnesium

Magnesium is a mineral that is abundant in the body. Most people are unaware of its numerous functions in ensuring physical and mental well-being Magnesium, on the other hand, is not as common in our modern diet of processed and flavored foods

It used to be that so many people had a magnesium deficiency without even realizing it.

They are aware of it. A 2017 study examined 18 previous studies magnesium study, the researchers concluded that

Magnesium does, in fact, have an anti-anxiety effect. This is the case because magnesium affects our muscles, brain, and heart

It is part of the nervous system and regulates a part of the brain known as the hypothalamus. The hypothalamus controls two brain glands.

These glands are known as the pituitary and adrenal glands in charge of controlling your anxiety levels Aside from anxiety,

There are numerous other compelling reasons to prioritize health. Magnesium concentrations can help with muscle pain, for example.

It can help you get a good night's sleep and improve your mood maintains normal blood pressure and can be used to treat migraines.

If you want to start by increasing your child's magnesium intake,
There are foods you can incorporate into their diet that are beneficial.
Magnesium is abundant. These foods include kale and other leafy greens. I avocado, spinach, legumes, dark chocolate, nuts, and seeds, and limiting myself to whole grains if you're looking for ways to reduce stress,
And anxiety naturally, you can try increasing your magnesium intake in your child's diet, or talk to a doctor about taking a supplement.
Magnesium is a true super mineral (Ferguson, 2019; Attitude, 2019). 2016).
Aside from focusing on these beneficial nutrients, it is critical to understand the risks of a high-sugar, processed-food diet
Your child is suffering from a mental or behavioral disorder. Sugar causes havoc in a child's system who is troubled by their mood, behavior, or hyperactivity, and eating only refined carbohydrates can lead to
Expect to get very little zinc from the snowy white hamburger.
You just gave them a bun to eradicate. Following an 80% whole foods diet and
A 20% what-kids-love-to-eat approach can help to balance things out nutritional issues you were unaware of that could lead to behavioral enhancement

The Rule of 80/20

Children do not want to be on a constant health journey, so if you are focused on providing them with a nutritious eating plan, the 80/20 principle is a great way to treat them every now and then. The 80/20 rule states that you should eat well 80% of the time and treat yourself 20% of the time. It's the ideal ratio for staying healthy and satisfied. In practice, this means that the kids can have a small-to-medium-sized candy bar once or twice a week, and the family can have pizza and ice cream on Friday nights. The remainder of the week will be spent eating nutritious foods. If you think my 20% is a little thin, which it may be, you can increase the treats slightly. It's critical that your children enjoy both healthy food and treats, and if they're still young, you have the upper hand. Because habits are difficult to change as a child grows older, it is easier to teach good eating habits to young children. If your child is used to eating more junk food, they will rebel if you try to implement the 80/20 rule. But don't be discouraged.

Nutritious foods can also taste good; once they're off the preservatives and salt, and their taste buds have returned, they'll be more compliant. Play with the 80/20 rule by asking your children what they want for treats each week. Just make sure they understand the relative size of the treat, and you'll have a happy bunch on your hands. If you want to learn more about clean eating and whole foods, keep reading to learn about the clean eating philosophy and how you can magically transform some junk food favourite into whole food options.

Philosophy of Whole Foods and Clean Eating

What do all of these expressions mean? Is clean eating and whole foods something you practise? Or are they essentially the same idea? I believe I am confusing everyone, including myself, so let me begin again:

"Whole foods" are foods that have undergone minimal to no processing, such as fruits, vegetables, whole grains, and legumes. Animal products, on the other hand, can be classified as "whole foods." The issue arises when attempting to classify foods that are not completely processed but are also not completely 'whole.' There appear to be several stages or layers of processing that result in very few foods being 100% whole food — only those plucked directly from a tree, in fact. This is because even simple processes like washing and chopping are considered processing, just as canning and preserving foods are.

However, there is a significant difference between simply washing food and canning it; with canned foods, preservatives and additives are added to make them last longer. This is the crux of the distinction; not all food processing procedures are created equal.

In fact, the terms "minimally-processed" and "ultra-processed" were coined to aid us in our confusion.

Food that has been minimally processed is food that has undergone processing that has left it close to its natural state. In this case, washing is a good example; dirt and pesticides were removed from the food, but nothing was added to change the composition of the food itself. This also means that if the food is only minimally processed, it retains the majority of its original nutritional value. As minimal-processing progresses to ultra-processing, ingredients such as salt, sugar, and fat are added, reducing the nutritional value of the food.

This basically means that while it is impossible to eat a completely clean diet, eating foods that are minimally processed and still resemble their most natural state is the best way to provide the most nutrients from food to your family and children who need to focus on nutrients and nourishment. Here are some examples of simple whole food substitutions for previously processed options:

Instead of using white bread, opt for whole grain or whole meal bread.

Replace the Cheerios with a bowl of steel-cut oats topped with fresh banana or blueberries.

Substitute a handful of unsalted mixed nuts for the snack bar.

Instead of purchasing protein from the deli section, try to stick to fresh, free-range chicken.

When you go shopping again, choose fresh fruit over fruit juice because it contains more fibre and has the right amount of fructose per serving.

Other options include substituting brown basmati rice for white basmati rice and attempting to make something from scratch rather than purchasing a ready-made version. There isn't always enough time for this, but every small step counts. Furthermore, teaching your child to love whole foods from a young age is likely to make the habit stick as they grow older, resulting in strong and healthy adults. Think about the 80/20 rule and have some fun in the kitchen. 2017 Health Agenda

Hobbies and productive activities

When we talk about productive activities and hobbies for children and teens with ODD, we mean activities that will help to subdue the aggression and defiance while also promoting a sense of physical and mental relief, decreased anxiety, and an improved mood. Exercise is one of the most extensively researched natural treatments for depression and anxiety because it is a low-cost alternative to expensive therapy sessions and, in some cases, medication. However, research on exercise has discovered that while normal low-intensity movement may keep a healthy person mentally fit, when an individual suffers from a condition or disorder such as depression or anxiety, a higher intensity level of exercise is required to achieve the same benefit.

This is most likely due to a person's brain's inability to produce enough of the required neurotransmitters when performing the same amount of exercise as a healthy person.

The Advantages of Organized Sports

Participating in organised sports is one of the best options available when it comes to the requirements you have for exercise, your child or teen's activities, and hobbies. It's almost like a treatment plan designed specifically for a child with conduct and behavioural issues.

Let's look at the general benefits of sports for children without taking into account the possibility that they have a disorder like ODD:

Aside from being an excellent way to stay active and exercise at both high and low intensity levels, there are numerous other advantages that parents should be aware of. There are team sports and individual sports, and each has its own distinct characteristics. The trick is to choose the right sport for your child, which can help change their attitude, outlook on life, how they react to rules and boundaries, and their overall development as human beings. Let's start with the general benefits of sports that apply to all children and teenagers.

Children, particularly those who begin playing sports at a young age and continue to play throughout their childhood, are more likely to have well-developed vision and are less likely to develop vision problems. Playing sports, of course, is one way to keep your child healthy and help them maintain a healthy weight for their age. According to research, children who are physically active, particularly those who participate in an activity after school, are more likely to maintain a healthy weight. Then, simply by learning to play and participating in organised sports, your child will be able to develop and fine-tune their coordination and motor skills. Motor skills and coordination are useful in any situation, including driving a car, and children who have participated in organised sports generally have a very well-developed sense of coordination and good motor skills.

Then, if you find a sport that fits your child's dynamics and personality, the sense of team spirit and positive relationships they will develop with teammates and coaches can help them develop self-identity and self-esteem. It's almost like recreating the dynamics of family teamwork at home, and it also has a very rewarding goal for kids when they work together and achieve their team's goals. What a priceless quality to learn that can help a child grow into an adult with a healthy mindset that will take them far in life.

What remains? So, amusement and friendship! This one may be difficult for your ODD child or teen because they are likely to show disrespect to their peers. However, if they can find friendship in this venture, it will change their lives.

How do you choose a sport that is right for your child after considering these benefits, which are applicable outcomes for all children who participate in organised sports? First and foremost, they must be enthusiastic about participating in sports. My little one liked karate because she thought it was all about fighting. To her surprise, it had nothing to do with fighting and everything to do with restraint and respect. Nonetheless, she was willing to make the mental shift because she enjoyed the sport's educational and physical aspects, so I knew we had found the right activity for her. She would be calmer, more open to suggestions and instruction, and sleep better after I picked her up from a lesson. However, that is not why we are here. We're here to focus on your child's health, so let's go over our options.

When considering different sports options, the first thing to consider is what your child or teen is generally interested in. Even better, if your child is interested in a specific sport, this can make the process go more smoothly. On the other hand, just as some girls enjoy watching football, being interested in or enjoying watching a specific sport does not imply that you want to play that sport. So, let's delve a little deeper.

What do you believe is your child's most pressing mental or emotional need right now that can be met by participating in sports? For example, if your child is not interested in team sports, it may not be worthwhile to investigate these options, and you may find better results by investigating options such as tennis, squash, track, or another type of sport in which your child competes as an individual. Individual sports are appealing to some children because the emphasis shifts from teamwork to developing an inner sense of individual drive, which can be beneficial in teaching perseverance and self-belief.

It is also critical to consider only sports that are appropriate for your child's abilities. Some children, for example, have co-occurring disorders such as ADHD, or they may have conditions such as asthma that affect which sports they are compatible with. It is critical to inform the coach about your child's or teens medical conditions, whether mental or physical. When you and your child have decided on a sport to try out for, put the foundation or sports organisation in charge of organising and training through your own assessment process. In relation to the sports club or organisation that you and your child want to join, ask yourself the following questions:

Is this program's vision and mission aligned with yours, or are there conflicts between your beliefs and those of the programme or organisation?

What level of parental involvement does the organisation anticipate from you?

Do the practice and game schedules correspond to yours and your child's?

How do coaches choose team members? Do you agree with the selection procedure and believe it is fair?

Is adequate supervision provided, and do the coaches and management team appear responsible and experienced?

Is the programme well-organized, or does it just happen?

Finally, does the programmer or organisation have insurance that will cover any injuries sustained by your child while training or playing?

If any of these points are of interest or importance to you, I recommend making a list of selection criteria and using it to find the best organisation or club for your child to join. Most of these criteria may not be necessary if you live in a smaller area and the setting is more informal, but you know the majority of the people involved. You can select which ones to use (Stanford Children's Health, 2019).

Sports have been shown to be particularly effective and therapeutic for children and adolescents with ADHD. Because ADHD and ODD are so closely related, researching the advantages can provide some final insight into the physical and mental advantages that have been documented through research and ongoing studies.

Athletic abilities have been described as an "island of competence" that your child can use to develop resilience and self-esteem that will help them cope with their diagnosis. Individual sports that focus on developing and mastering a specific skill are especially beneficial for children with ADHD. Martial arts, swimming, archery, ballet, and even diving are examples. This focus element is excellent for improving their concentration and focus, and the physical aspect assists them in getting rid of excess energy. One of the most beneficial aspects of sports for a child who has been diagnosed with a disorder is the sense of achievement and accomplishment they gain from it. There is no equivalent to how valuable this is for the development of their self-worth and self-esteem, which can be the reason they lash out in many cases (CHADD, 2018).

Attempts at Art

Art and other expressive activities can also be very therapeutic for children with ODD. Similarly to how you express yourself physically when you play sports, some children or teenagers may be better suited to expressing themselves emotionally or artistically. You can either talk to your child about taking an extracurricular art class or take them to an art store and buy some supplies for them to experiment with at home. Create a small art space for them to practice their creativity if possible. Acrylic paints are a good choice because they are water-based and dry quickly, as opposed to oil paint, which takes forever to dry and is difficult to clean once it has messed up. You can also get them a set of drawing pencils, charcoal, a sketch pad, and one or two canvasses. They can buy an eBook with tutorials or watch YouTube videos on how to create landscapes, seascapes, impressionist paintings, realist images, and so on.

When they've finished something you know they worked hard on and are proud of, frame it and hang it on the wall where everyone can see it. This act of gratitude will boost their self-esteem tremendously.

Writing a Tell-All I believe that all children who are emotionally and psychiatrically challenged should keep a diary. In fact, everyone struggles, so keeping a diary can benefit everyone. Some people simply enjoy writing more than others, just as some people prefer painting to others.

Writing is another therapeutic way to release pent-up energy that may have been unfairly projected on a family member. Purchase a nice diary for your child in the same way that you would have purchased proper art supplies for them. Buy them one with a cover they'll like; one they'll look forward to opening and writing in every day.

Also, include a special pen. You can even make an agreement with them that whenever they feel like acting out, they must first write down their feelings in their diary before acting out. Tell them that the diary is theirs and that no one will read it, so they can write whatever they want as long as they write how they are feeling at the time.

It doesn't matter if the diary looks a little worn after a few months. When it's full, tell your child to put it somewhere safe and get them a new one.

Reinforcement Learning

While we're on the subject of raising healthy ODD munchkins or larger versions of them, consider how to encourage them to develop healthy habits. Using behavior modification techniques is one way to sneakily work on changing your child's or teen's habits. I know it sounds like you'd have to strap your child to a chair, apply electrodes to their forehead and temples, and then press a big red button. However, the simplicity of reality may surprise you.

Positive reinforcement is an extremely effective way to modify the behavior of your ODD child or teen. From the perspective of an ODD child, they usually expect a scolding, reprimand, or punishment as a result of their destructive behavior. So, how does this method work if it does not involve strapping them to a chair or any other type of furniture and is still effective? Positive reinforcement has been shown to improve misbehaviors such as being aggressive to others and breaking or violating rules. It also promotes socially acceptable behaviors such as following directions and (willingly) sharing with others.

Another reason to use positive reinforcement is to help your child develop a sense of responsibility by having them do their chores, complete their homework, and get along with other family members without arguing or being difficult. Let's take it one step at a time and begin with the theory of genius.

Would you get up every day and probably work late once or twice a week if you didn't get paid at the end of the month? I'm not talking about volunteering for non-profits here — I'm referring to the typical primal 9-5 daily grind that most people go through in order to put food on the table, minus the occasional feel-good moment when you show your colleague how to plug in their computer. Let me tell you, I most emphatically will not. What's the point of all that blood, sweat, and tears if there's no reward or payoff? What is it called that 'thing' that keeps us going to work every day? That is, in essence, positive reinforcement. It's another word for remuneration in adult terms, but how does it translate into ODD child/teen language?

To begin, children, like adults, are wired in the same way; if they receive positive reinforcement for their good behavior, they will continue to do so. The same is true for hard work; knowing that they will be rewarded for it will motivate a child to maintain a certain standard in their work. Here are some examples of how you can use positive reinforcement in simple ways for younger children to more subtle and complicated ways for older children and teens who want expensive items:

Cheering and clapping will have an effect on the children. A teenager may think it's the most ridiculous and embarrassing thing that's ever happened to them, which I find quite amusing.

Depending on the situation, a good high-five can go either way. However, avoid high-fiving your teen in front of their friends. They may, however, value it as a private moment of celebration between the two of you.

Because of its affectionate nature, hugging is an excellent way to reinforce your child. This approach will work well with children and will help to satisfy their desire for affection and attention. An ODD child may resist this type of affection at times, but in the context of achievement and approval, it is almost always a huge success.

Here's something you can do with your teenagers. It entails spending some quality time together. Of course, your child wants to go out for ice cream, but you can also take your teen out for lunch, dinner, or coffee. Take the time to laugh and say encouraging things to your child. As well as a slice of cherry pie.

Why don't you try talking positively about your child to another adult in front of your child? "Jenny painted the most beautiful still life yesterday," for example. She even designed and arranged the still life herself! I'm going to have it framed for my living room." Your child will feel as if he or she is the most important person in the world!

In other cases, you can provide them with tangible rewards or additional privileges — this works well with older children. For example, as a reward for good behavior or compliance with house rules, you can extend your teen's curfew by an hour. You could also give your child more TV or video game time.

Praise

Praise is also a fantastic way to use positive reinforcement, and there are various ways to use praise to increase its effectiveness. Kids frequently act out because when they exhibit any form of good behavior, it sometimes goes unnoticed, making them feel as if they are working in vain. We can't really expect a child to do their chores for the greater good, can we? The irony is that negative behavior receives the most attention from parents, despite the fact that it should be the opposite. Which of two children would get your attention if they were gallivanting around the house, but one was jumping on and ruining your new leather couch while the other was sweetly building a Lego castle? I believe we will all begin by frantically attempting to get the wild one off the couch. The other, on the other hand, deserves to be recognized for their good manners. What if you flipped the script and focused on praising the good behavior while ignoring the couch-hopping? In no time, there would be two children sitting quietly and playing with Legos. If you give your child positive feedback about what they're doing, they're more likely to act out, and by using this technique on an ODD child or teen, you might be able to influence their pattern of outbursts to become less frequent and even reduce the triggers that cause them.

Behaviors that respond well to praise are very similar to those that respond well to positive reinforcement; this is likely due to the fact that verbal praise is a type of positive reinforcement. Let's look at some behaviors that are particularly responsive to praise:

First and foremost, there is prosocial behavior. If your child or teen is willing to take turns without fighting, use positive or kind words, share with others, and generally cooperate with others, these are all actions that respond well to praise, and praising your child in these situations can create a pattern of reinforced behavior. Then, if your child exhibits any form of compliance, which is usually a rare occurrence if you have an ODD child or teen, this behavior will respond positively to praise. Compliance can include following general rules, following instructions given by an authoritative figure, or simply going about their business when they could have been engaging in naughty and destructive behavior.

Finally, when your ODD child shows that they are making an effort; even better if they are making an effort to improve in areas that need improvement, this should be acknowledged and praised. Even if they aren't quite there yet, recognizing and applauding their efforts will encourage them to keep trying and staying strong.

Now that we've looked at situations where praise works well, it's time to focus on strategically applying praise to get the most effect and reinforcement. Surprisingly, if praise is not given appropriately, it can be detrimental to your child's perception of themselves and their abilities, which can be harmful when they enter the world as adults. By looking at the examples of healthy methods below, you will most likely see the unhealthy ones as well.

First, give realistic praise. We all believe that our children are the smartest, most beautiful, and most special children on the planet, but telling them this too frequently may be detrimental to their development. Instead of saying, "Maggie, you are the best ballet dancer I've ever seen," try to identify and focus on an actual positive feat that you can encourage. Change it to "you really did a great job with your pirouettes; I can tell you've been practicing hard!" for example. If the compliment is specific to an aspect or technique that your child has been working on, they will feel even more validated and loved because they know you've been paying attention and have noticed the improvement.

Constructive praise entails avoiding labeling your child, which is closely related to the preceding approach. Labeling is simply a shortened version of giving exaggerated or general praise. Even if this is your honest opinion and your child has an IQ of 140 or higher, referring to him as "Mommy's little genius" is counterproductive. My old high school friend decided to become a medical doctor, and when her mother refers to her or speaks about her, she doesn't call her by her name; instead, she refers to "my daughter that's a doctor." Each and every time. Which do you think your child would prefer: for their parents to recognize them as a person or for them to be identified by their well-known profession? This is an example of how, despite your best intentions, this type of praise can go horribly wrong and actually be harmful to your child.

Then, to get the most out of praising your child, be specific in your praise. Most of us say "great job," assuming that our children understand what we mean.

However, enunciation influences how a child interprets praise.

You can either say "well done" or "well done for remembering to take out the trash!" Personally, I'd prefer the second option because I already know what I'm being praised for.

Now, here's an intriguing one I heard while socializing with other parents with children. It's almost as if the concept of praise isn't fully grasped. A parent would complement their child but include a negative phrase or connotation in the message. It reminds me of how my grandmother handled praise; when I told her I got a good grade on a test, she responded, "Well, now you can make it even better next time." Is there any kind of praise in there? I never told her about my test results again. As a child, a good score was not explicitly acknowledged in the praise, but I later realized that it was implied.

However, implied praise is insufficient for a child. It's the same as giving praise, which should be a positive experience and message but is laced with negativity or scorn. "I'm proud of you for not attempting to ruin dinner," for example. The duality in that sentence will not motivate your child, and their attention will be drawn to the latter part of the sentence, which contains negative language. "Oh, Mom or Dad thinks I always ruin dinner," your child will most likely think. Great." This could backfire and result in negative reinforcement. "I'm proud of you for being so positive and chatting with everyone at the dinner table tonight," you could say instead. What are your thoughts on this? Have you ever caught yourself providing your child with negative praise? When dealing with an ODD child or adolescent, your child's repeated misbehavior and aggression can program your brain into a negative copilot mode, and negative words will then spontaneously leave your mouth, even if you want to communicate a positive message. This is entirely understandable. So, parents of troubled children, such as children and teens with ODD, should pay attention to this specific aspect of how praise can be effective if used strategically.

Finally, when focusing on children with behavioral disorders, you can boost their self-esteem by praising their effort rather than the outcome. Although the outcome is not always successful, you can always commend your child for making an effort.

They will be motivated to increase their efforts, which will eventually lead to success. How proud can a parent be of a child who perseveres even when things are difficult? They deserve to be recognized and praised by those who care about them the most (Morin, 2019).

Constructive Family Time Planning

There are many things you and your family can do to organize some family time, depending on what everyone enjoys doing, and focusing on activities that will improve family dynamics and relationships. Here are some objectives to consider when looking at various family activities:

First and foremost, the activity should fit into your family's team goal or vision. For example, if one of your goals is to improve sibling relationships, planning an activity that promotes this goal is ideal.

Second, planning an activity that everyone will enjoy will be extremely beneficial. Your ODD child, and especially your ODD teen, may act as if nothing interests them, but don't be fooled. Observing your child's daily activities will give you a good idea of their interests, likes, and dislikes.

Finally, strike a balance between the types of activities you want your family to participate in. Try not to schedule all of them at home or in front of the TV, for example. Change the scenery by going outside or doing something active. Have some fun with your family! Consider the following examples as a starting point for your own authentic activities:

A Movie Night with a Difference

How old is everyone in your family? Do you have teenagers or tweens? Are there some opposing viewpoints on everyone's favorite movie? I know what it's like to want to fall asleep while watching a movie that everyone else loves. Movie nights, on the other hand, can be enjoyable bonding experiences.

If you have tiny tweens, your movie options will be more limited, but otherwise, each family member gets to search Netflix, pick a movie, and put all the movie titles into a hat. If you don't have a sturdy hat, use a plastic container. Make sure no one can see the names by writing them on paper and folding it in half, leaving the blank sides visible. Then, set aside a day every week or every other week for the family to get together for a movie night — no excuses!

Make one person's favorite snacks each night (you can make a separate hat containing everyone's preferences and draw one each time if you want), place the mattresses on the floor in front of the TV to ensure there's enough room for everyone, and get comfy. You can even decide to wear your pajamas to every movie night. Concentrate on having a constructive conversation and making sure that everyone's opinions and comments are given equal weight.

Maintaining Activity

There is no better way to teach your children the value of nature than to load them all into the car and take them on a family hike. If you live near scenic nature reserves or hiking trails, this is a great family activity that will also get everyone some exercise. You can incorporate activities such as bird watching, photography, and learning about the various trees and plants that grow in your area. Go swimming or tanning if there's a lake nearby — your kids will love it. You can play games and have a picnic on the beach.

If you're only going for a hike, you can also bring a picnic or take everyone out to lunch when it gets too hot to be outside. If it's winter, you can take everyone ice skating — there's so much to do outside. Please be cautious if you want to go on one of those extreme family team-building activities where everyone slides off a cliff. And remember to stay hydrated!

Let's Make a Difference!

This is a highly recommended option. It will teach the entire family a lot about giving back to society, appreciating each other and what you have, and inspiring you to work even harder to become a close-knit group of people who love and respect one another.

Volunteering is not something that many people do, but organizations such as homeless shelters and animal shelters are always in need of volunteers. Even nursing homes will always appreciate a helping hand, not to mention the elderly residents who haven't seen their relatives in a long time.

Making a difference in the lives of others, especially your ODD child or teen, can teach you a lot about yourself. For example, they may recognize that they face many challenges in life, but they also have many things to be thankful for, such as a supportive family, a roof over their heads, and a delicious meal waiting for them when they get home from school. It's truly heartwarming to be compassionate to others.

If your children enjoy animals, take them to a shelter where they can interact with and feed the animals. Some animals become extremely stressed when kept in a small enclosure for an extended period of time, so if you have older children or teens, arrange for them to take the animals for walks or play with them outside their enclosures. How will it feel for a child who despises authority and automatically rebels against it to work with those who have so much less than they do? It can have a significant impact on their frame of reference, and the entire experience can strengthen you as a family.

The Dinner Club

Right now, I could use some pizza. Not the kind that's delivered to your door in 15 minutes, but the kind that you make in your own kitchen, starting with the dough, chopping up all the toppings, and watching it slowly cook in the oven with your mouth watering. Do you and your family enjoy pizza? Have you ever attempted to make your own pizza at home? It's the best because you can put whatever you want on it.

Making dinner with the entire family and turning it into a family tradition is a productive way of strengthening family bonds, and there are activities for all skill levels, from washing the vegetables to frying the bacon and kneeing the dough.

However, you are not required to make pizza. That was just the first thought that came to mind, probably because I was hungry. If your family has a favorite cultural dish, what a great way to bring everyone together to work as a team. The best part is getting to enjoy the feast that you all worked on afterward.

Take Note, Lovely Parent

These activities are intended to be enjoyable, empowering, and emotionally beneficial to your family. You are constantly aware, however, that you have a child or adolescent present who can blow up, defy instruction, and act negatively. As a result, it is critical to maintaining control of the situation at all times. If it's just you and your partner, you can work together to keep the atmosphere as you want it. It is critical to use positive reinforcement equally on all of your children and not make it obvious that the entire operation is "Operation ODD." Your children may pick up on this, and their reactions to your positive efforts may turn them around and worsen the situation. If you have an ODD child or teen, this is one of the most important things to remember. Before you begin implementing some of the behavioral techniques we discussed, you will be walking on a razor's edge, not knowing when, why, or how the explosion will occur. What makes you a powerful parent is your ability to rise above this, to recognize that it is something that can happen, and to work toward making a significant difference in your child's life.

Chapter 7
How Should I Discipline My ODD Child?

Or adolescent

This has happened to all of us. We've tried several approaches with the Attempt to discipline our ODD child or teen without becoming emotionally involved angry, agitated, or simply out of control if you've done a lot of work, You may have done your research and tried a variety of approaches have tried one that would eventually work, but the difficult part is to stick to it when your child or adolescent is being so difficult And the most vexing and perplexing aspect of dealing with an

Even though you, as a parent, must deal with an ODD child or teen, remind yourself that it is a condition and that your child's destructive behavior is normal. and abrasive behaviors are not who they are, they still appear to know exactly when and how to push your buttons and will never let you down When they lash out, they are hesitant to do so.

This is why ODD parents are exhausted, defeated, and sometimes depressed even completely depressed; try to wrap your mind around that

It is not easy to live with a paradox, and parents who deal with it daily know this should be commended for actively attempting to comprehend their child's behavior situation while being constantly attacked There are two essential components of successfully disciplining an ODD child or adolescent The first is employing techniques that are effective and are not Your child will suffer emotionally as a result of this. Second, and most importantly, parents struggle because consistency is so difficult. Don't Leave even a small gap for your child to identify and fill take their chances with acting out Consider these fundamentals first strategies you can use in your home to tame your children by severely restricting their opportunities to express their aggression and anger misbehave.

Fundamental Approaches

Let us start with the facts. Children and teenagers with ODD are outright disrespectful, confrontational, and disobedient. So, how do you stop this destructive behavior that affects everyone in your family? Understanding their behavior and reacting accordingly is critical.

Positive Attentiveness

To begin, one factor that can exacerbate ODD behavior is if the child observes that they are negatively reprimanded more than their siblings. This essentially means that their brain will wire itself to believe that their siblings always get positive attention while they always get negative attention, which can lead to feelings of bitterness or jealousy, which will worsen their behavior. So, if you notice your child or teen misbehaving, try to stop what you're doing and give them your full attention for at least fifteen minutes. Try to smother the aggression and defiance with positivity and affection, and depending on their age, do a quick activity with them or ask them to do something special for you. This approach is nearly identical to the one we previously discussed, in which the child's negative behavior is completely ignored.

However, you will use this approach if you know that the behavior is due to neurological interplays, such as ADHD acting up, or if you can see that your child was clearly triggered.

The Behavior Modification/Reward System

The second strategy can be successfully combined with the first to form a multifaceted prevention strategy. The second strategy is to develop an action and consequence behavior plan with your child. This will work well if your child is old enough to understand the concept, but given the age range of children diagnosed with ODD, your child is unlikely to be too young.

Begin developing the strategy by identifying the behavioral issues that must be addressed. Acting aggressively towards you, your partner, or siblings, refusing to follow orders or do schoolwork, shouting or saying nasty things, throwing tantrums, or misbehaving at school are all examples of these issues. After you've identified the critical behaviors, you must devise appropriate consequences that aim to improve your child's understanding of their behavior while not undermining their self-esteem. There could be rewards for good behavior and extra chores for bad behavior. A reward system has been tried as a disciplinary strategy for ODD children and has proven to be effective time and time again. There are various types of reward systems that parents employ, and many parents develop their own unique ideas and systems that meet the needs of their household. However, there are systems that already have established procedures and rules, such as the token economy system, which works well with ODD children and teens; as an example, consider this reward system.

How to Implement a Token Economy System in Your Home

A token economy system is known as one of the most effective ways to get any child, including children with ODD, to follow your house rules. If your child has ODD, there may be a slight delay in compliance, but success has been demonstrated. This system functions similarly to an action-and-consequence behavior plan, but it includes a built-in rewards system. Your children will earn tokens for achieving specific goals on a daily, bi-daily, or weekly basis, and the tokens will function almost like a monetary system that they can use to claim or purchase larger rewards. If your child is still in kindergarten, consider using a sticker chart because they enjoy this format; however, if your child is older, tokens work well. Assume you want your child to finish their homework in the afternoon, come home from school without any complaints from their teachers, go a week without throwing a temper tantrum, or do their chores. They can earn tokens for performing their duties, and these tokens have a monetary value. You can have a system linked to earning the tokens that indicates what they can "earn" or which rewards they can get with x number of tokens. These rewards can begin small for a small number of tokens and grow more valuable and desirable as the number of tokens increases. By selecting rewards that you know your children will enjoy, you will motivate them to behave, collect the tokens, and save up for their rewards. So, where do we begin if we want to build a token economy?

Maintain simplicity. Parents can get very excited about creating a rewards system or a token economy system, which can result in a lot of planning and an elaborate setup that looks almost like a business pitch! The issue is that it will completely perplex your child. Approach the creation of the system from your child's point of view; you know your child better than anyone else, so as long as you remember that the system is being created for your child and why your efforts will most likely be wildly successful.

- You must now decide what objectives your child must meet in order to earn tokens. Pour yourself a glass of wine and think about it for a minute. You don't want your child to believe that some good behavior is more valuable or "better" than others; instead, you want to give the impression that all good behavior is equal. You can focus on effort if you want to give your child tokens of different values for different goals without creating this impression. Alternatively, all tokens can have the same value, and your child will simply have to save for longer in order to receive larger rewards; it doesn't have to be that complicated.
- Next, an important factor to consider is not focusing solely on bad behavior and setting difficult goals for your ODD child. They will struggle with the majority of their behavioral goals, and they will require motivation by earning tokens for other behaviors or activities that they find easier to complete or achieve. So, when creating goals for your ODD child, make sure that there is one easily attainable goal and some intermediate goals hidden in between. Depending on your child's age, you should also think about how many behaviors you want to include in your system at once and whether your child will find a system with multiple behaviors or activities confusing.
- This point is simply a reminder to remember the most important requirement when dealing with an ODD child: positivity. This system, like every other aspect, must be approached positively, and "difficult" goals should not be framed as reprehensible or repugnant behavior. Your child's behavior indicates the amount of negativity they are experiencing within themselves, so the more positivity you can surround them with, the better. Assist them in viewing these behaviors

as aspects that can be improved rather than traits they have because they are bad people. Every goal in the token economy system has the same value; however, you may want to consider implementing your own interpretation of the rewards based on how much effort the child needs to put in to achieve it. Also, if you want to use the effort component to generate tokens of varying values, the concept of effort must be logically quantifiable. An incorrect interpretation of the effort here would be that Annie worked "twice as hard," so she received a token with a higher value. Avoid using abstract concepts when calculating and estimating rewards and tokens because children struggle to understand them.

- When a child earns a token, be present to give it to them in a contractual manner. If you handle this part of the process by telling your child, "Go get your token; it's on top of the fridge," you're missing an important step; the step in which you physically acknowledge your child's achievement, which is critical to the systematic improvement of their behavior.

- Another useful idea is to assist your child in identifying a special designated token container. This will be especially effective with younger children because it will make the entire concept more official and legitimate. You can go all out and decorate a jar or container, add a label, and put it somewhere in the house where everyone can see it, or in your child's room if they prefer.

- Choose a type of token that your child cannot find anywhere in the house and add it to the token jar secretly. If you use marbles as tokens, your child may be able to steal some marbles from a friend and secretly place them in the token jar. We're not saying they'll do it, but you know how kids are. Poker chips are an example of a token that can be used. You can also make your own tokens; just make sure your child cannot access them.

- If you want your token economy system to be less materialistic, think about creating rewards that don't cost money or aren't based on monetary status.

- Giving your child the latest PlayStation, for example, is likely to create the impression that they will expect something even bigger the next time. Keep this in mind as you consider which rewards to give your children. The rewards can also teach them a lot about life and that money isn't everything. However, you still want them to reap the benefits; otherwise, the entire token economy concept may fail.

- Although a token economy system is generally very successful when used with ODD children and teens, there may be some difficulties at first. You can prepare for the most common token economy system issues ahead of time, so you'll be ready to fix them if they occur. One of the concerns you may have had while reading this discussion is that your child may be uninterested in earning tokens because they dislike the rewards being offered.
- If this is the case, consider discussing the rewards with your child and reaching a compromise that does not cross any of your boundaries, such as a set amount of money or something you are willing to do. If your child has a lot of privileges and is used to getting what they want, it may be difficult for them to understand the token economy system. Allowing them to play video games, for example, can be used as a reward.
- Don't exclude your other children from the token reward economy system if you have more than one. You can instill healthy competition and relationship-building in your children by advertising the system as a positive way for them to collaborate and by assigning each child an easy, intermediate, and difficult goal to achieve. There may even be challenges in which your children must work together to obtain their tokens, which you can refer to as a "group challenge."
- Finally, depending on what you have available and what you've already made available to your child, try to provide a variety of rewards throughout the weeks, as children can easily become bored.
- You can assist them in managing their "reward wealth" by using the tokens now for smaller rewards or by giving them larger rewards that they must save up for, implying long-term good behavior.

Make Unambiguous Rules

Your ODD child most likely enjoys complaining and arguing about rules because they provide a convenient platform for an argument or a tantrum. They are also usually very vigilant when it comes to parents enforcing the rules — if there's a loophole somewhere, they'll find it, and you'll know the second they suspect something is unfair. So, this is a separate component from any rewards system you decide to implement in your home; it is about establishing ground rules. To avoid "you said, they said" situations, make a rule card or document outlining all of the rules and place it near the fridge or the back door where the entire family can see it.

If you want the rule list to be effective, keep it short, treat it with respect, and treat a family member who breaks the rules with respect. Include basic rules such as chores, schoolwork, and family communication. Finally, make sure you don't break any of the rules and then dismiss them — this will sabotage any attempt to get your ODD child to understand why they have to follow the rules.

Don't Give In to Power Provocation in a Conflict

If you have an ODD child or adolescent, you are well aware that your authority is regularly challenged. Children and teenagers with ODD enjoy and excel at entangling authority figures in ongoing arguments or debates about what they perceive to be unfair or inconvenient.

However, if you have a solid rule system that applies to everyone in your household, there is no need to engage your ODD child or teen in such a lengthy debate about their interpretation of right and wrong. There's no need to respond to unproductive power struggles if you've discussed the house rules with the family, including all of your children, and all necessary questions have been answered.

Here's an example of what you can accomplish. If you give your ODD child or teen a clear instruction, such as washing the dishes, and they try to argue back, if you are confident that your instruction was clear, move on to the consequence set for that action. Your child will argue with you about washing the dishes because it will keep them from having to go to the kitchen and wash the dishes. Don't be fooled by this delay tactic; make sure your child understands the instruction, and if they don't, remind them of the consequences before enforcing it.

The goal here isn't to force your child to do something they don't want to do, but rather to maintain fair and reasonable household rules. Giving them negative attention will feed their reactive tendencies, so simply remind them of the house rules and enforce them if they do not do their part. When it comes to dealing with ODD effectively, you have two best friends who will always have your back: positivity and consistency (Morin, 2020b).

Continuity, Continuity, Continuity

It cannot be overstated. ODD children thrive on loopholes, inconsistent behavior from authority figures and even peers, and taking advantage of opportunities when they see them. Your system should be as watertight as Noah's ark; however, instead of holding out water for forty days and forty nights while meandering through the great floods, yours should hold tight until your child reaches their adolescent years. That's what I mean by "tight ship."

Taking all of this into account, your ODD child is not the only component of your life, and you have other priorities, many of which have been discussed in previous chapters. Slipping up is unavoidable. Making errors is unavoidable. If your child becomes aware of this, they will use it as a trigger to react and misbehave because, despite the fact that they have been systematically weaned off toxic behavior through your positive and consistent approach, they still have a psychiatric disorder and are neurologically wired to act that way. Don't let it bother you. Stop it in its tracks by continuing as you were before it happened.

People make mistakes, but your child is not yet in a position to understand this.

Calm Down Your Hyperactive Child

When an ODD child or teen is on the verge of doing something aggressive or losing it completely, we usually respond with a negative word like "no," "don't," or even a phrase like "stop that." At this point, the child is so sensitive to their own emotional instability that simply saying 'no' to them can send them over the edge. Yes, the word no is negative for most of us, but if we are told 'No,' we will most likely comply and not be triggered by its negative nature. Not an ODD child or adolescent.

As with many of the scenarios we've discussed in this book, parents do their best to prevent and assist, but their methods only seem to exacerbate the problem because of the small details we overlook. Nobody can deny that ODD is similar to rebellious behavior, but it is much more complicated. And what if you say no, don't, or "stop" a rebellious person? The opposite reaction is likely.

Here's a technique that will make you laugh. Hopefully, your child will laugh as well, because that is the goal! Use a code word instead of words that convey negative reinforcement, such as 'no' and the others we discussed earlier. You can choose a word without discussing it with your child, or you can choose a word together so your child can use it to warn you when they are about to have an episode. Imagine noticing your child blowing up and turning red in the face because they have to take out the trash, and instead of using negative language, you simply look at them. Their jaws may drop to the floor. This can be your code word for all negative reinforcement words. "Remember dear, swigglypoo," you say when you see that mouth open in protest. "But mom," you might say. "I said, SWIG-GLYPOOOOOO." They'll figure it out in no time.

Alternatively, you and your ODD child or teen can collaborate by selecting a code word, and your child can alert you when they anticipate an aggressive episode. This will necessitate a conversation with your child, which can be a positive experience for them. Allowing your child to choose the word empowers them, and then you can discuss what should happen if they give you the code word. Should you, for example, go for a quick walk around the block? Or perhaps you should go shoot some hoops.

To make my child laugh, I would simply put on loud music and start dancing like a crazy person. They'll be dancing with you before you know it.

Collaboration with your child's teachers and school

If your child is not being homeschooled by you or your partner, you should discuss their condition with their teacher or teachers, as well as any other individuals who should be aware of the potential complications. This is because an ODD child is often a special needs child when it comes to learning, especially if they have co-occurring conditions such as ADHD, language learning, or cognition issues. For example, whether your child is attending school online or in person, you can request that any distracting items in the background of the online classroom, such as multicolored posters, be removed. If your child must sit in a classroom, you can request that they be seated in the front, where they will not be able to see as much movement from the students behind them.

Making class activities very structured is another example of something small that can make a big difference in an ODD child's behavior, and it will work extremely well if the teacher can provide a large planner on the wall in a physical classroom where all the students can see it or a digital one the teacher and your child have access to in an online setting, which indicates when they are going to do what during class. This structural modification is critical and can save you a lot of arguments and conflict in the classroom.

It may be difficult to discuss all of your child's requirements with their teacher, but they may not have dealt with an ODD child before, and while it may appear to them that you want to change their teaching style, the majority of the information you provide them is to make their day as conflict-free as possible. It's critical that they understand this because if they don't and find your approach to be too controlling, they may consider ignoring your advice entirely, which they will regret for a long time. I'm bringing this up now because the next topic you might want to discuss with a teacher is how they communicate with their students. Instead of providing information and expecting students to accept it for what it is, it is far more prudent to engage them in the discussion, especially if an opinionated ODD student is present.

By taking this approach, the teacher allows the ODD child to have a healthy release, reducing the likelihood of a buildup and subsequent explosion later.

The next suggestion is for the teacher to include an emotional regulation program or lessons that actively focus on teaching children how to deal with strong emotions such as anger and frustration.

This is simple to arrange if your child attends school online; however, if this is not the case, you may need to arrange a meeting with the school staff. You can also inquire about bullying and well-being programs that teach children how to be resilient in the face of adversity.

Finally, it is critical that the teacher or teachers understand the necessary balance of rewards and punishment. It is pointless if you, as a parent, have a great and healthy system in place at home, but your child's teachers at school do not focus on rewarding your child at all because they are only concerned with their bad behavior. It's like putting your child through school only to have them fall apart again. Always ensure that, whether your child attends school online or in a physical setting, the teacher understands the importance of positive reinforcement for your child's well-being (raisingchildren.net.au, 2020).

Siblings Must Be Empowered

If your ODD child or teen has siblings, they are most likely experiencing the same stress and aggression that you are. Having an ODD child and other children will require you to not only divide your focus but also to turn each eye into a super-powered laser beam, at least at first, when a system is not yet established and your household is relatively chaotic.

Why Is It Difficult?

Because your ODD child is constantly on a mission to control everything, the nature of the relationships between ODD children and teens and their siblings resembles a constant power struggle. Sharing, considering the wants and needs of others, and playing nice are not likely concepts in their minds, and these concepts will have to be planted and cultivated with care and patience. Meanwhile, you must consider your other children's well-being, and it is critical that they understand the situation without retaliating in a confrontational situation by bullying your ODD child due to their condition.

Siblings may react in these ways as a result of the high levels of stress and frustration they face. We can all understand as parents that this is not a healthy environment for them, and it can cause feelings of resentment if they believe their ODD sibling gets away with misbehavior without being properly punished. Because of the hurt and anger, they are feeling, they may feel neglected and rebel against how the household is run. When children fight, it is common for parents to let them sort out their issues or differences on their own. However, when one of the siblings has ODD, this is not a wise strategy. Your intervention is critical because they take conflict and aggressive behavior to a whole new level and have no interest in resolving the issue.

Show them how to look for signs.

One strategy you can teach your affected siblings is to recognize the warning signs and then completely stop communicating with their ODD sibling. "Have you noticed what your brother does before he throws a tantrum?" you can ask your child. "Yes, he balls his fists and gets red in the face," your child may say. If you notice your child has identified these warning signs, instruct them to simply turn around and walk away. "I know it's difficult because your brother's anger frustrates you, but if you just turn around and walk away, he won't have anyone to fight with."

Avoid saying things like, "You'll be a better person if you turn around and walk away." This will give your child the wrong impression, and the best way to show your children that they are important is to avoid using language that implies you prefer them over your ODD child or teen.

Provide Them with Options

Another important message you should convey to your children is that it is acceptable for them to set boundaries and recognize and respect the boundaries of other family members. They can assert their emotional and physical boundaries, and they can notify another family member if they enter that space without their permission.

Because their ODD sibling is only aware of their own boundaries and not those of others, your children need to hear this from you as their parent. This is a method of empowering your children by telling them that they, too, have a rightful place in the household, but that they must deal with an invasion of space or a crossing of boundaries in a non-confrontational manner. This should not be used as an excuse to fight with their ODD sibling.

Redress

You will mean a lot to your affected siblings if you make fair restitution. Making fairness a priority in a household with an ODD child will help the siblings feel worthy, experience fewer feelings of resentment, and give them a sense of belonging. This redress is, of course, intended to be reciprocal, and your children should understand that. So, if one of your siblings is at fault, restitution will be applied in the same manner as if the culprit was their ODD sibling. This should be done in a stoic manner, with emotions not dictating the actions taken in such a situation, but rather the actions themselves. For example, restitution or redress should not be done with the attitude of "oh, it's you this time, isn't it?" Make your face into an unreadable blank slate so your children can focus on your actions. If you do this the first few times, your house may explode with bombs. Just keep up the good work. You demonstrate your love for your child, so no guilt feelings are permitted!

Applaud the Initiative

When you begin implementing new rules in your home, you will almost certainly encounter resistance and possibly aggression. However, if you expose your children to a positive and proactive environment at home, there is a chance that they will develop the ability to solve problems on their own could have resulted in conflict situations. These attempts and successes should be celebrated because they show growth, especially if they involve communication between your ODD child or teen and a sibling. Praise their efforts and make sure they understand how they help your family achieve its goal of being a cohesive and loving unit (Abraham & Studaker, 2020).

Chapter 8
Increasing Your Child's Self-Esteem

Self-esteem describes how much a person values themselves and their self-worth in their world. It is critical to developing your child's self-esteem because a positive self-image makes them feel good about themselves.

Children who have high self-esteem are confident and competent.

They recognize their own worth and have faith in their abilities. They find fulfillment in the things they can do for themselves and will always go out of their way to do their best.

When children are confident in who they are, they are more likely to be open-minded, and they will encourage themselves to try new things while managing and learning from their mistakes. They are self-assured in their ability to advocate for themselves and will seek assistance from their guardians when necessary.

- Children with high self-esteem
- Consider yourself grateful.
- Are tough and satisfied when they know they have done their best
- Maintain self-control.

- Are you self-sufficient?
- Have faith in themselves
- Are pleased
- Children with low self-esteem:
- You may be dissatisfied, irritated, anxious, or unhappy.
- Failure anxiety
- Lacks self-assurance
- Self-doubt
- Feelings of inadequacy

How Does Self-Esteem Grow?

Children gain positive self-esteem as they achieve their goals and realize that hard work pays off.

Achieving things in life shows them that they have what it takes to realize their dreams and future goals. Their small victories provide them with positive reinforcement, and they develop the mindset that as long as they give their all, it is more than enough, even if they fail.

When children accomplish something, it delights others, such as their friends and families. These positive reactions also make them feel good, and they gradually gain confidence and self-esteem.

Children with low self-esteem are more likely to fail and receive little positive feedback from others. As a result, they are doubtful of themselves and their abilities. They may lose motivation and give up trying to do things because they are afraid of failing. They have a difficult time dealing with any mistakes they make, and they may refuse to accept the fact that they are worthy of success.

The 4-Step Plan for Increasing Your Child's Self-Esteem

Children with ODD already face a slew of behavioral issues, as well as rejection, loneliness, and, most likely, low self-esteem.

As parents, you must help your child develop self-assurance and confidence by identifying the small things in which he or she excels.

Creating a strong emotional bond with your child and rewarding them when you notice their determination, even if they do not succeed, will help them develop a positive self-image over time.

Each child is born with talents; some have many, while others have one exceptional gift. Even a child with ODD has amazing abilities, but they may be more difficult to discover because they are hidden. Even when they are discovered, your child may find it difficult to share them with the rest of the world. I'm going to reveal four secrets for raising your child's self-esteem and allowing them to become the person they were born to be.

Your child must understand from the start that you love them unconditionally. They will be subjected to a great deal of negative attention as they grow older, so now is the time to instill in them a sense of self-worth and belonging.

You must focus on their positive characteristics before they become another statistic or are labeled as bad or naughty. Pay no attention to the pathologists. They must place a child with a specific disorder in a box or category, failing to recognize the complexities, deep emotional connections, and essence of your ODD child's soul.

When a child is labeled as having a mental or behavioral condition, many of them lose their individuality. Read these four steps to help your child develop positive self-esteem and push past the boundaries of the ODD label.

Make and Maintain Connections

Connecting with our children is just as important for us as it is for them. We will have a healthy relationship if our children believe we love them and our bond is strong. We must remember that they look to us for guidance, that they require consistency in their lives, and that the only way to maintain a strong bond with our children is through daily habits of connection.

Give them physical and emotional attention. A kiss good morning or a hug goodbye. Happiness in the home should be a daily ritual that allows your child to laugh even at their mistakes or disappointments, which can lead to a disconnect if not addressed appropriately.

Turn off your phone and ask your child to step away from their technological devices so they can enjoy each other's company and have some family time. Communicate, relate to one another, debate or argue; even if you disagree, make an effort to connect. Go on family outings or simply take a walk on the beach.

Showing your ODD child how to bond and form healthy connections will ensure that they are not isolated and alone in life.

The Value of Recreation

Play is an essential part of every child's healthy development.

It fosters important life skills such as self-assurance and individuality. Play is a safe environment for practicing executive decision-making and developing self-confidence. Playtime allows your child to achieve their own goals, which will eventually boost their self-esteem.

Children make up their own rules during playtime. It gives them the freedom to do whatever they want and broadens their executive skills. They gain confidence as they are given more opportunities to make their own decisions.

Allowing your children to solve their own problems while playing allows them to seek out more play-based learning strategies on their own. Although it is important to challenge and inspire children while they play, we must also allow them to discover things on their own.

Improve Your Problem-Solving Skills

Your child will realize that they can solve challenges and difficulties on their own as soon as they begin to develop general problem-solving skills in their daily life. Once they have gained confidence, they must proceed to the next activity that is both challenging and important to them; they are on the right track. Every child can overcome any obstacle if they are reassured and guided by their parents or caregivers.

Remember that the only thing that matters is progress and improvement, not perfection.

Give Thanks

We are all aware of how important it is to recognize our children when they accomplish something for which they have worked hard. Self-esteem grows over time as children work hard to achieve specific goals and feel good about themselves when they do. What you say and how you say it as a parent will help your child recognize things they should be proud of. Praise also contributes to the development of a strong bond between the child and the parent or caregiver. Goal achievement is important, but you shouldn't focus solely on your child's achievements.

You should consider your child's feelings as well. If they achieve many goals but are unhappy or have a detached, unhappy childhood, their accomplishments will be meaningless to them.

Rather, ensure that you raise a content child who is confident, self-assured, passionate, sociable, and ethically righteous. This will ensure that their future is bright regardless of their academic achievements.

Getting Rid of Your Child's Low Self-Esteem

Every child, especially those with ODD, requires a sense of social and academic success, as well as the assurance of your unconditional love, regardless of their successes or failures in life.

Because they are constantly corrected and disciplined, most children with ODD or other learning disabilities develop low self-esteem. They begin to believe that they are a failure who will never be clever enough. We all know that these feelings of disappointment are unfounded, but we must support our children and highlight their strengths in order to boost their self-esteem.

Adverse Reactions

Everyone has a ceiling. When they had had enough and responded negatively to a situation without thinking before speaking. Children with ODD can drive their parents insane with their defiance and bad behavior, and we can get so angry that we yell at them or say something that makes them feel terrible afterward. We might even avoid our children entirely.

We must consider why we find it difficult to communicate with them in a peaceful and loving manner. Is it because your child's restlessness, inattention, or rash actions are too overbearing, and if so, is their ODD being treated adequately?

How are they doing in school? Could they be suffering from undiagnosed educational issues? If your child's ODD behavior is eliciting negative reactions from you, other relatives, or peers, you must consider the impact on his self-esteem.

George's Life Story:

George, a child with ADHD and ODD, was displaying concerning behavioral and psychological issues at home and at school.

His parents did not believe in medication or any behavioral techniques recommended by a trained professional. His teacher suggested that he undergo a mental evaluation, and after the necessary tests, George was diagnosed with ADHD and ODD. George began to make significant progress at school and at home after being placed on the appropriate medication in conjunction with the appropriate behavioral methods to treat his ODD. He would still exhibit behavioral issues on occasion. It was later discovered that when he did something wrong, his parents would yell at him or make snide remarks. After attending family therapy, both parents realized that the way they communicated with him was not only damaging his self-esteem but also making him feel like a failure. They have since changed their attitudes and the way they communicate with one another, and the family is now achieving great success.

Academic Achievements

The majority of children with an ODD struggle in school. Because they were not informed of your child's disorder, their teachers may perceive them as disobedient and disruptive. Discuss your child's condition with their teacher in an appropriate manner. They may be having difficulty with things like attentiveness or participation during a lesson. They may become agitated or aggressive as a result of their overall academic difficulties.

Ask the teacher for feedback on any behavioral issues your child is experiencing, and explain how a change in the educator's approach might help. Perhaps all your child needs are better management during school breaks and in between classes. When they begin to daydream, they may only require minor assistance to refocus. A learning disability does not preclude a child from succeeding in school; it simply means that they require more attention from their teachers than the average student.

If your child is on medication, talk to their doctor about alternative medications that may help with their school issues, or talk to their psychologist about additional therapy options to improve their awareness and concentration.

The Importance of Peer Relationships

One aspect to consider is effective education. Another important area in which you should assist your child is peer relationships.

Making a connection with a classmate is extremely difficult for children with ODD.

Keep an eye on your child when they invite a friend to play. Take note of their actions. For example, are they nervous and concerned about playing games with their friends? Do they struggle to understand social cues from their peers? Do they become too preoccupied, impatient, or hyper to engage in play with others?

Do they avoid any type of physical activity because they lack gross motor skills, such as kicking a ball? Can they grasp the concept of working as part of a group? Do they struggle to concentrate when playing board games?

Once you've identified your ODD child's specific social issues, you can start looking for solutions. They may need to seek additional treatment or attempt a physical activity for which they are not physically prepared in some areas.

Building positive self-esteem takes time and effort, but when you see your child's smile when they start participating and mingling with their peers, you'll know it was all worth it.

Active Praise: Boosting Your Child's Self-Esteem

You'll be surprised at how praising your child's positive behavior, no matter how minor, can help them develop their self-esteem.

When you express your delight when you observe positive behavior, you encourage your child to keep up the good work rather than revert to negative patterns. Just a few words of encouragement can boost your child's self-esteem, reduce negative behavior, and strengthen your two-way emotional bond.

It may appear simple to say a few encouraging words when your child is behaving well, but what if your child has ODD and you only notice their negative behaviors? Our natural reaction is to scold or reprimand our children because we believe this is the only way they will recognize their mistakes and learn not to repeat them.

The problem is that when we only focus on the negatives, we increase the likelihood that their undesirable behaviors will continue, which will eventually harm that already fragile emotional bond.

The trick with an ODD child is to focus on even the smallest positive behavior. Praise communicates to your child that you noticed their good behavior and expressed your delight. Descriptive praise differs from ordinary praise. When you use descriptive or effective praise, you don't just tell your child that you're happy because they behaved; you explain to them exactly what actions made you happy and why it's important for them to continue doing so. Children require specific instructions. Descriptive praise explains exactly what is expected of your child and reduces uncertainty or misunderstanding.

Here are some examples of effective or descriptive praise:

Discovering Something Positive

When your child is having a tantrum or being aggressive, it can be difficult to find something positive to focus on. Instead of telling them what not to do, tell them how happy you are that they did not act out their aggression physically.

Describe the positive behavior you want them to emulate.

Using the aforementioned example, we can teach our children that it is never the right thing to do to harm others.

Explain to them that if they are unhappy or angry about something, they should come and tell you why so you can decide what to do together.

Encourage Your Child to Behave Well

Telling your child that you are happy when they are not aggressive will not motivate them to stop. Instead, explain to them that if they hurt anyone, they will lose privileges such as TV time, and they will have a reason not to do it. If they resort to violence instead of approaching you as you requested, you must follow the consequences you specified. As a result of their wrongdoing, their television privilege will be revoked.

Reward Positive Behavior

Rewarding your child for positive behaviors is an excellent way to encourage productive behavior. It doesn't have to be a toy, ice cream, or chocolates; you could give them more TV time, allow them to ride their bike outside for five minutes longer, or even choose a family activity for the weekend. When you start noticing positive aspects in your child's behavior, they will begin to recognize these traits in others, and soon the entire family will use effective praise.

Boosting Self-Esteem in Children with

Concentration Difficulties

Children with behavioral and psychological disorders have a difficult time focusing. They are impulsive, have difficulty dealing with authority figures, and become defiant when forced to follow rules. This can be extremely difficult for educators. Giving kids consequences or threatening them with expulsion will only lead to feelings of inadequacy and embarrassment. To help an ODD child who lacks focus thrive, explain to them that you admire their determination even if they get easily sidetracked. You can use some of the following approaches to help them cope with feelings of irritation, hopelessness, or uncertainty that frequently accompany concentration difficulties:

Determine the Cause of the Problem

When your child exhibits aggression or frustration, it is not because they are intentionally being mischievous; rather, they are likely to be overwhelmed by something they are struggling to achieve or handle. It is your responsibility to investigate the reason for their behavior. You can assist them if they don't understand certain parts of their homework or if a school project is simply too difficult to complete.

As soon as you identify the issues causing their reaction, you can discuss them with your child's teacher to assist in breaking down the overwhelming school material.

Divide large problems into manageable chunks.

How do you handle a massive problem? You divide it into smaller, more manageable chunks. Because an ODD child has difficulty focusing, break a large project down into smaller tasks. Children may require the support of a parent or educator, as well as some sort of framework to follow. Help them with one question, for example, and then tell them that you will be nearby to help if they need it, but they must solve the rest of the problems on their own. Maintaining your cool when working with your ODD child on their problem on a regular basis has a reassuring effect on them, and they will work harder to complete their schoolwork or projects.

Checklists Are Effective

Most of us keep a diary to keep track of our days. Make your child create a detailed to-do list. When they can mark a task as completed or completed, it makes them feel more accomplished.

Maintain Eye Contact and Communicate

When faced with difficulties in their schoolwork, preoccupied children tend to freeze. To ensure that there is always someone to help them when they need it, you must be proactive and remain involved with both their homework and their educators.

Enable but never empower

Children who have difficulty focusing frequently believe they will never be able to succeed on their own. We overcompensate as parents by doing their homework or projects for them, but this only reinforces their sense of failure. Tell your child that you are confident that they will succeed if they try.

Stay in the Present Moment

Children with poor concentration already have racing thoughts. A reward in the near future will not motivate them to work harder. They require something tangible to hold onto right now. Tell them that as soon as you two finish your schoolwork, you can go out for ice cream. This will encourage them to give their all in the present moment.

Make use of previous victories

When your child becomes agitated because they are struggling with something, try to remind them of a previous situation in which they succeeded. Ask them to consider which strategies they used to succeed in the past and which strategies they can apply to this specific problem.

Before They React, Intervene

Intervene as soon as you notice the beginnings of a temper tantrum before it escalates into a major drama. Look for telltale signs or changes in body language that indicate they are becoming irritated so you can calm them down before they lose control.

Maintain your calm and stability.

No matter how frustrated you are, never raise your voice.

Yelling makes your child jittery and anxious. Rather than attempting to control the situation, try to explain your expectations in a gentle manner. A calm demeanor always works wonders.

Demonstrate Empathy

Children who are easily distracted already feel inadequate in all aspects of their lives. These children require extra care, inspiration, and understanding. Show compassion and make an effort to keep your child motivated. Many times, all your child requires is a sympathetic ear to listen in order to feel better about themselves.

Increasing your child's self-esteem can help them cope with mistakes and make them feel proud and independent.

Chapter 9
The Positive Parenting Plan in 9 Steps

As a parent, you always want what is best for your child. But sometimes we forget to look our children in the eyes while trying to understand what they are going through. Your hectic schedule eventually catches up with you, and you find yourself on the proverbial "short end" of the parenting stick, with your patience dwindling.

In such situations, keep in mind that you are your child's guide, and your actions can have an impact on them.

However, because the dynamic of your interactions with your child can change quickly, it is always best to be aware of certain things. After all, the path to bettering your child's behavior begins with you.

Proper Parental Characteristics

We all want to raise a healthy, happy child, but many of us are unsure how to approach our parental roles. Do I just go with the flow, or do I employ parenting techniques similar to those used by my parents?

Whatever your parenting style or parenting concerns are, you must help your child develop understanding, morality, independence, self-discipline, compassion, collaboration, and joy. Here are a few parenting traits to consider in order to encourage your child and assist them in achieving their life goals.

Don't force or demand; instead, lead and support.

Parents should never force a child to do anything under any circumstances, even if you believe you are only gently pushing them to do their best; they will most likely do the opposite and quit entirely. You can never give a child too much love or support; show them that they can rely on you when things get tough and that you are a confidant.

Discipline is essential.

Make and enforce rules. If you do not manage your child's behavior when they are young, they will struggle to learn self-efficacy. The rules that your child learns at home will shape the rules that he or she applies to themselves later in life. Keep in mind that there is a distinction between discipline and punishment. Children who lack discipline are typically unappreciative, and materialistic, and will struggle to make friends and be content as adults.

Everything is absorbed by children.

Whether it's bad language, inappropriate behavior, or how you treat others, your child is watching you and will mimic your every move. Remember that every action has a reaction, so before acting on impulse, consider the consequences. To teach your children respect and empathy, you must always be on your best behavior.

Never be obnoxious, vindictive, or hostile.

It is natural for people to be irritated or annoyed, but when we become abusive or degrade others, we teach our children that it is acceptable to be condescending and mean. It is critical to instill in your child the importance of treating others as they would like to be treated.

What, where, and who

As a parent, you must be aware of where your child is, who they are with, and what they are doing. By asking these questions, you should not feel like you are micromanaging your child; you must ensure their safety and keep them out of harm's way, regardless of their age. Their job is to learn, have fun, and have a good time during their childhood. It is your responsibility to ensure that they do so.

Encourage Independence

Of course, rules and limits are necessary for your child to learn self-control, but you should also encourage them to be independent so they can learn self-direction. True success in life is achieved by striking a balance between the two. It is common for children to strive for self-sufficiency, and children will strive for independence because it is part of their human nature to want to feel in control of their lives. Remember that it is okay to help your child with something if you are teaching them to do it on their own eventually.

Show Them You Care

Make time for your children, inquire about their day, and truly listen to them. Even if it's just a five-minute conversation in the car after school, the only thing that matters is that you keep strengthening that bond between you and that they feel truly loved.

Accept Your Child for Whom They Are

Live in the present moment and focus on your child, not on what they will become in the future. It is natural for parents to want only the best for their children. To ensure that their children have everything they never had, remember that your child is an individual, and they may enjoy activities that you disliked. So don't force them to participate in events they don't want to. You can suggest that they try something to see if they like it, but you should never live your life and unfulfilled dreams through them.

Attend and talk, talk, talk.

Being involved in your child's life and a hands-on parent takes time and effort, and it frequently necessitates rethinking and reorganizing your priorities. You may have to sacrifice your own needs to accommodate your child's requests, but if you are present mentally, emotionally, and physically, you will be amazed by the connection you build with your child and will learn things about your child that you did not know before. Do not stop talking or listening to one another. Have a conversation with your child rather than just talking to them.

Teach Respect your child will learn to respect others if you treat them with respect.

Explain to your child that they must treat everyone with the same respect, love, empathy, and charity that they expect in return.

Speaking to them about gratitude and remember who they are as individuals are far more important than what they will achieve.

9 Steps to Parent a Child with ODD
Improve your ODD Self-esteem as a child

Infants develop their own personalities as they grow, but as babies, they perceive the world and themselves through the perspectives and behaviors of their parents. Many children mimic their parents' mannerisms, expressions, and even the way they speak.

Everything you say and do as a parent has an impact on your children's self-image development. Praise your children for even the smallest accomplishments so they can gain confidence and pride.

Allowing them to complete tasks on their own will increase their independence and demonstrate to them that they are capable of accomplishing anything they set their minds to. Never be condescending, and never compare your child to others. This will exacerbate their sense of insignificance.

Negative statements or remarks such as "You can be so stupid sometimes!" or "You are such a spoiled brat!" can be more painful than any physical injury.

When your child makes a mistake, think before you speak and be sympathetic. Explain to them that everyone makes mistakes and that even if you disagree with their behavior, you will always love them.

Make Time for Your Children

We as parents are so preoccupied with work and life these days that we don't have the luxury of spending hours with our children. It doesn't mean we're bad parents; it just means we need to prioritize the time we have wisely. Spending quality time with our children is essential if we want them to grow up to be well-rounded, happy people.

A great road trip or an expensive activity does not constitute quality time.

You can have a great time eating dinner together, playing a board game, or simply putting together a puzzle. Getting a movie they enjoy and having them help you prepare snacks to eat while watching it together is a great way to bond. Even assisting with homework allows for more opportunities to spend time together and bond.

Children who do not receive attention from their parents must frequently overreact and misbehave in order to gain their attention. Remember that any attention is preferable to none, so even negative attention will suffice.

Regardless of how hectic your schedule is, make sure you spend some quality time with your child every day to talk, bond, and get to know one another.

Positive Behavior Should Be Recognized

Reduce the number of negative and harsh reactions you have to your children on any given day. Make sure you don't criticize them too harshly.

Instead, compliment them more frequently to boost their self-esteem.

Every day, make an effort to find something to compliment. After the compliment, please give them a hug or kiss. You'll notice after a while that you're encouraging the kinds of behaviors you want to see in your home.

Sometimes we are unaware of our hostile reactions to our children. Instead of applauding their good behavior, we may disapprove of the majority of their actions. Even if we have the best intentions, our constant reprimanding may give our children the impression that we are their boss rather than their parents. Every positive action you notice, identify and praise it, and remind your children how much you love and appreciate them. Mentioning all of your child's positive characteristics will encourage them to do their best in everything they do. Compliments, rewards, and acts of love are essential for effective parenting and improving your ODD child's behavior.

Be a Good Example

You'll be surprised at how your actions influence your child. Children believe that their parents' behavior is acceptable. So, before acting aggressively in front of your children, consider the possibility that your child will act similarly when they are angry. Children who imitate aggressive behavior typically have a parent or role model who exhibits this type of behavior at home.

Modeling appropriate behavior is the most effective way to be an effective parent. Children will imitate appropriate behavior if you do.

Be truthful, approachable, humble, caring, and gentle at all times.

Remember to treat your children the way you would like to be treated.

Maintain Consistent Discipline

To teach discipline, you must set limits and restrictions as a parent. The main goal of disciplining your children is to instill self-control qualities in them while also teaching them to distinguish between acceptable and offensive public behavior.

Your children will occasionally test the boundaries you set, but as long as you set limits that have consequences when broken, they will quickly realize that you mean business. Begin with a warning, followed by a time out, and finally, take away an activity they enjoy, such as playing games. Consistent consequences also ensure that your child understands what to expect if they do not follow the rules you have established for them.

Fine-tune Your Parenting Approach

You have a significant influence on everything your child does and thinks as a parent. Every parent has their own parenting style, which can be defined as how you communicate with your child and how you discipline them. As your child grows older, so will your parenting style. There are four main parenting styles, and we will go over each one briefly.

Permissive Parenting:

Parents who are too soft can be identified. They may say that they will punish bad behavior, but they almost never follow through. They will only become involved if the child is blatantly disobedient. They're quite lenient, and children with ODD can easily persuade them to reverse any consequences imposed.

The Uninvolved Parent:

The uninvolved parent has no idea or only has limited information about their child's movements, friends, and whereabouts. These parents have few if any, rules, and their children are left unsupervised and unguided.

The Authoritarian Parent: An authoritarian parent places a premium on strict rules and total compliance. They are uninterested in communicating with their children and expect their children to do as they say, with no exceptions.

This approach is the best of all the parental styles mentioned.

Authoritarian parents have rules and consequences, but they also listen to their children's opinions and prioritize their children's feelings while remaining in charge.

Authoritarian parents are devoted to their children, putting in the time and effort to prevent bad behavioral complications from becoming uncontrollable. They also employ constructive discipline methods to reinforce positive behavior in their child. As a result, we are raising happy, accountable, and efficient children who have no trouble sticking to positive choices and avoiding dangerous situations.

We understand that ODD children can be difficult, but if you remain diligent, and loving, and apply the appropriate type of discipline, you will notice small, subtle changes.

Always communicate effectively.

Remember the adage, "don't just hear someone, and listen to them?"

To help your child learn and develop good communication skills, as well as healthy, strong family connections, you must actually listen to them. Positive communication with your child will boost their self-esteem because they will feel that their opinion is valued. Positive open communication allows your child to communicate with you when a difficult situation arises in their life. Kids have valid points and opinions, and they deserve proper explanations if they ask for them. Be forthright and forthright about your expectations. If there is a problem, define it, tell them how you feel about it, and solicit suggestions from your child to help you find a solution.

Make sure to punish bad behavior, but first, listen to their side of the story. If your child knows they can come to you with an issue and that you will understand their reason for doing something if they tell the truth, your child will come to you directly when they need guidance and support. Negotiation is also necessary. Children who feel a sense of ownership over a decision are more likely to stick to it. So, come up with appropriate consequences for bad behavior as a group.

Confirm Your Unconditional Love

When it comes to adjusting your child's behavior and guiding them in the right direction, you have control as an authority figure. You can accomplish this by showing them unconditional love regardless of what they do. This is not to say that you never give them consequences or discipline them. It implies that when you do discuss their behavior, you should never make them feel guilty or too critical. Don't undermine their self-esteem; instead, try to encourage self-regulation and reassure them of your love.

When disciplining them, make sure to express your disappointment in their actions, not in them. Soothe them and assure them that you will always love them regardless.

Determine Your Parental Needs and Limitations

There is no such thing as a perfect human being; instead, accept your flaws as a parent and work on the things you want to change in both yourself and your defiant child.

Prioritize the aspects of your household that require the most attention first, and then address the remaining issues separately.

There is no shame in admitting when you are overwhelmed.

Take occasional breaks to do something that brings you and your partner joy. Putting yourself first does not make you selfish; it simply demonstrates that you are human. Another important lesson you can teach your children is to take care of your own happiness.

Let's take a look at how you can change things as a parent to support your children one by one.

Chapter 10
Medication and Treatment, Therapies of Various Types

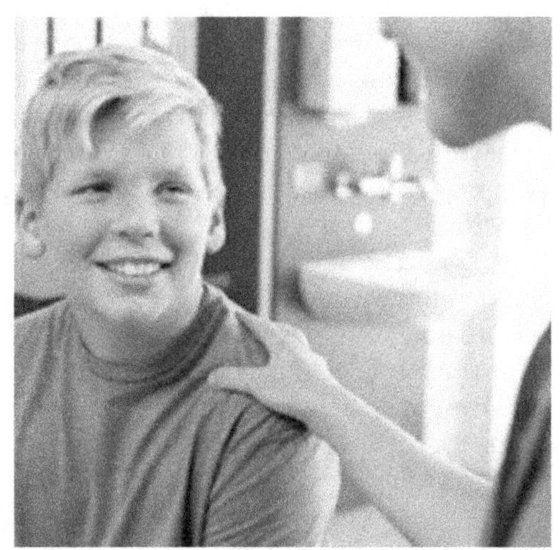

Medication: Certain medications can help children and adults with ODD when used in conjunction with PMT or when PMT is not an option. Mood stabilizers, antidepressants, anti-anxiety medications, stimulants, and antipsychotics are the most commonly used drugs. It should also be noted that these medications are not always used on children, and if they are, they must be closely monitored by a doctor who is familiar with the side effects and how the medication may interact with your child's body, mind, and/or personality. If a child's long-term behaviors are severe enough to warrant a diagnosis of ODD, the doctor will most likely prescribe mood stabilizers, which are used to control aggressive and impulsive behaviour.

You should talk to your child's doctor about whether it's a good idea for them to take ODD and PMT medications. The doctor may believe that because your child is young, it is not a good idea for them to use medications, but many children who use PMT also require the assistance of medications to see improvement in their behaviour. Sometimes parents will try to develop their own methods for ODD treatment, and while these methods may have worked for other children their age, they may not be the best option for your child.

Treatment for ODD

ODD, like other mental and mood disorders, is treatable, and there are so many treatments to choose from that you may not know where to begin. Furthermore, taking the "start at one point and work our way through them until we find one that works" approach can do more harm than good, not only to your child's or teen's mental state or condition, but also to their self-esteem. Imagine jumping from treatment to treatment and being told that none of them are working on you. That would make me even more dissatisfied and angry with the world, and it could provide an opportunity for an ODD child or teen to justify their behaviour.

All mental health treatments will involve some trial and error, but you want to minimize it to the greatest extent possible by first being informed and then arming yourself with the most up-to-date information available. Now that we've discussed the nature, symptoms, manifestation, and coordinating disorders associated with ODD, let's move on to the available treatments, what each type of treatment can offer your child or teen, how they differ and may be similar, and why one would choose a specific type of treatment in specific circumstances.

Why can't ODD be cured?

Treatment can assist you and your child in managing the oppositional defiant disorder, but there is currently no cure. The fact that medical experts do not know what the cure is or why it is not curable may be due to the fact that they are unsure and cannot pinpoint an exact cause. ODD appears to be caused by a combination of factors, including environmental, neurological, and even genetic components. Similarly to how researchers and medical practitioners are aware of the influential and contributing factors that can be linked to an individual's proclivity to develop oddly, they are also aware of therapeutic and psychiatric treatments that can alleviate symptoms but not completely cure them.

Treatment for ODD is primarily psychological and in the form of psychotherapy, and some can be used alone while others can be used in conjunction with other treatments. Your child's treatment may also be affected by the presence of a co-occurring condition, which may alter the approach or techniques needed for effective treatment. The following section discusses the most common types of ODD treatment and how they work.

Treatment Options for ODD

If you are a parent of an ODD child or adolescent and are looking for treatment, know that there are many different ways and methods to treat ODD. Speaking with a therapist and allowing them to get to know your child may also allow them to identify a type of treatment that will work best, which is preferable to select one at random.

Cognitive-Behavioral Therapy (CBT)

Cognitive behavioral therapy, or CBT, is a psychotherapeutic treatment that teaches people how to identify and then change disturbing or destructive patterns of thought that negatively influence their behavior and emotions. This means that cognitive behavioral therapy aims to change negative thoughts that occur automatically and cause or worsen emotional problems in a person's life, which can be linked to depression and anxiety. According to research, spontaneous negative and even harmful thoughts have a negative and unfavorable impact on an individual's mood.

The simplest way to describe the CBT process is to identify three steps during the therapy. The negative or harmful thoughts are first identified, then challenged by the individual who experienced them with the help of a therapist, and finally replaced with more realistic and objective thoughts.

The concept or philosophy of CBT is based on the recognition of thought patterns. CBT employs a wide range of strategies to assist individuals in changing their thought patterns. Role-playing, mental distractions, relaxation techniques, and journaling are some examples. Aside from the fact that there are many different techniques, there are also different types of cognitive behavioral therapy to be aware of. These 'types' are also related to how they differ methodically, despite sharing the same philosophy or principles. All of the types involve relevant techniques aimed at addressing emotions, thoughts, and subsequent behaviors, and each has a distinct focus due to differences in methodology.

As previously stated, cognitive therapy is based on identifying and changing distorted or unrealistic thought patterns that result in related emotional responses and subsequent behaviors.

Dialectical behavior therapy (DBT) aims to address thoughts as well as the emotions and behaviors that follow. However, it employs strategies such as mindfulness and emotional regulation.

When dealing with thoughts and behavioural issues, Multimodal Therapy requires you to address seven interconnected modalities. Sensation, behaviour, affect, imagery, cognition, interpersonal factors, and biological or drug considerations are examples of these modalities.

Rational emotive behaviour therapy, or REBT, involves first identifying irrational beliefs, then actively challenging the identified beliefs, and finally moving to a state of recognition and change to improve thought patterns.

After reading through all of the different types of CBT, it is clear that, while they may take different methodical and therapeutic approaches, the goal remains the same. The benefit of different types is that one approach or therapy type may be more compatible with one type of person than another. Even if two people have the same disorder, there are more tailored ways to approach and treat them.

CBT is typically used as a short-term treatment, but it can effectively treat and improve symptoms in an astonishingly wide range of disorders. All of these disorders may be caused by negative or irrational thought patterns.

Personality disorders, panic attacks, anxiety disorders, bipolar disorder, addictive behaviour, anger problems, phobias, and stress control issues are some of the conditions that benefit from CBT. Instead of sitting back and only listening, the therapist takes an active role in the therapeutic process and works hand-in-hand with the patient during CBT. CBT is intended to be a goal-oriented therapy in which patients collaborate with their therapists to achieve mutually agreed-upon objectives. The person is not kept in the dark about what CBT entails, and he or she is aware of all aspects of the therapeutic process.

CBT's impact stems from the idea that thoughts and feelings play an underlying and fundamental role in one's behaviour.

For example, a person who constantly thinks about car accidents and searches for information about them online will most likely develop a fear of driving and avoid even taking a ride in a car. However, such a person is not always aware that they have these obsessive thought patterns, and even more so, that they cause certain negative or unrealistic reactions or behaviour. This is where CBT's effectiveness comes into play. Helping someone become aware of these persistent and influential thoughts paves the way for the next step, which is engaging with and understanding them. This process may be difficult for a child or adolescent with ODD, especially if they are still young, so explaining it to them is critical.

CBT has been empirically proven to work on individuals who exhibit toxic behaviours, and it is typically a less expensive treatment option. Here are the CBT steps that lead to successful change, as well as two situations that can stymie or negatively impact CBT progress:

The first step, as previously discussed, is to identify negative thoughts. First, the individual must recognize the power of their thoughts and how they influence their emotions and behaviour. If the person undergoing CBT struggles with introspection, they may require additional support because this is a critical component to the identification of toxic thoughts and a new process of self-discovery.

Following that, new skills that supplement and reinforce positive behaviour must be identified and implemented. Individuals undergoing therapy will eventually be required to practice these skills in real-life situations, which will begin as a rehearsal process and will eventually result in the formation of a new neural pathway that will cause a natural tendency toward coping mechanisms and healthy behaviour.

Goals must be set in conjunction with the implementation of these new skills and coping mechanisms. Without goals, these positive reinforcement behaviours will progress but not reach their destination.

The development of problem-solving skills is also an important component of CBT. Problem-solving is a component of critical thinking, and it will benefit your child from an early age. Although they will not be able to identify all problems because objectivity is difficult for a child, you can help them systematically develop this life-changing skill with the help of a therapist. Teenagers will not have as much difficulty developing problem-solving skills, though they may require a push in the right direction.

After you've digested all of this, keep in mind that the transformation will be gradual, if not slow. Rushing your child or teen's mental transformation may have the opposite effect; instead, give them a reason to work hard toward their goal. Tell them how much you appreciate them.

Therapy for Parent-Child Interaction

PCIT, or parent-child interaction therapy, is a combination of behavioural therapy and play therapy that works well for younger children and their caregivers or parents. Throughout the therapeutic process, the adult learns new skills and techniques to help them cope with children who have behavioural problems or disorders, emotional issues, language disorders, mental health issues, or language issues. This type of therapy focuses on the adult, teaching and empowering them to develop coping mechanisms and improve their communication with a troubled child, which can include physical and verbal exchanges.

PCIT was developed for a specific age range, which is from 2 to 7 years, and if you compare it to the description of cognitive behavioural theory, which we discussed previously, you'll immediately recognise why this may be one of the more appropriate choices for younger children. CBT, for example, focuses on the patient and allows them to go through an introspective process that a child of 2-3 years would not understand. PCIT, on the other hand, gives parents control and training in changing potentially triggering behaviour and interaction with their young children.

Parents play with their children in one room while the therapist observes and then coaches them in an adjacent room separated by a one-way mirror during the PCIT process.

Using an earphone device, the therapist and parent communicate during the play process to ensure that the parent's responses are specifically tailored to the behaviour the child exhibits during that activity. This also creates a very effective learning process, which would have been based on trial and error, but this element is not significantly reduced here due to the therapist's observations and leadership. A therapist would typically advise a parent to avoid using negative language and to ignore negative behaviour if it is otherwise harmless. To counteract this, they are encouraged to praise and be enthusiastic about any positive behaviours. Other skills include reflecting the child's language back to them, which aids communication, increasing the child's vocabulary by clearly and audibly describing the child's activities, and imitating their good behaviour to show approval.

In many ways, PCIT is a relationship-building process that takes place in a controlled environment where parents, who take the lead in this process, can learn new skills while practicing relationship-building. Improving your relationship with your troubled young child can lead to better behaviour, which can improve family dynamics overall. Long-term use of this therapy has shown an increase in the child's confidence, and a decrease in anger, resentment, and aggression, and it ultimately regulates healthy interaction between the parent and the child.

If you recognise any benefits in this description of parent-child interaction therapy that you believe may benefit your situation, specifically related to your child's age, you can find a qualified therapist by looking for a licensed mental health service provider with a master's degree or higher, and preferably additional training in PCIT. Furthermore, it is critical that you and your child form a bond with the therapist and establish a trusting relationship (Psychology Today, 2020).

Psychotherapy in a Group

Group psychotherapy typically involves one or more therapists working with a group of patients. This type of therapy can be used alone, but it is also frequently used in conjunction with other types of individual therapy and psychiatric treatment. Groups can start small, with three to five people, but larger groups of up to twelve people can also work, especially if the patients get along well. A psychotherapy group would typically meet twice a week for one to two hours per session. Group therapy sessions can be open or closed, which means that new members are sometimes allowed to join during the therapy period. In other cases, patients sign up prior to the start of the sessions, and the group membership remains the same.

A typical child therapy session may include musical therapy, art therapy, and play therapy. The format of the sessions is determined by the therapists' desired outcome and the patient's condition. Group psychotherapy for teenagers may involve more talking and sharing of experiences, but expressive activities such as art and music therapy will not be ruled out as therapeutic options. Therapists have a lot of leeway in how they want their sessions to go, and some can be structured while others can be more spontaneous and free-form.

Group Psychotherapy is used to treat a wide range of mental illnesses and disorders, but it always strives to provide the same benefits to its patients. One advantage that this type of therapy can provide for your child or teen is that they will be among peers while also being supervised by therapists. While therapists foster positive interaction, group members can offer support and encouragement by recognizing that their fellow members may be dealing with similar issues and struggles. This can help them feel less isolated than they would if they were alone at home experiencing these emotions and outbursts. This brings us to the next proof of group psychotherapy: it provides your child or teen with a safe space where they may feel they can say or express things they cannot say or express in front of you, at school, or at home.

Don't take this personally; it usually means they have some toxic feelings they want to get rid of that they don't want to expose you to, and if they are given an open and safe environment to do so, they can get rid of these pent-up emotions in a much healthier way. What occurs in the group remains in the group. What's more, for children or teens with ODD in a group setting, the therapist can pay close attention to how they interact with others and behave in a social setting, which is typically a problem for children and teens with ODD. Therapists can observe and provide valuable feedback on their behaviour.

Finally, group therapy is usually less expensive than cognitive behavioural therapy, which can have a significant role-playing effect in some households (Cherry, 2009).

Behavior Analysis in Action

One of the treatment options for aggressive behaviour and a lack of impulse control is applied behaviour analysis.

These are not disorders in and of themselves, but they are present in autism spectrum disorder, conduct disorder, oppositional defiant disorder, and intermittent explosive disorder, the majority of which are cooperative disorders, including our focal point, ODD.

Because of their ability to elicit an immediate reaction from their target, impulsive and aggressive behaviour are frequently viewed as behaviours that reinforce themselves in various social contexts. Because if aggression or impulsive behaviour is directed at you, your first reaction will be to address it, which means you gave the person projecting that behaviour the attention they desired. Of course, your natural reaction to aggressiveness or impulsivity directed at you will be negative and defensive, which only serves to reinforce that reinforcement. This is one of the reasons why changing aggressive and impulsive behaviours in children and teens is so difficult, and applied behaviour analysis focuses specifically on analyzing and constructively approaching these behaviours, and tackling them proactively.

If the behavioural issue has not been established, an applied behavioural therapist (ABA therapist) will generally follow a procedure with their patients. They will begin by determining which behaviours require attention and change, and then set goals or identify expected outcomes from the therapeutic process. Furthermore, the ABA therapist will decide which measures and techniques to use based on the individual situation, as well as how to measure progress and changes in a patient's behaviour.

Furthermore, the ABA therapist may teach the patient new skills or coping mechanisms, assess progress, and ultimately determine whether additional behaviour modification is required in a specific case. Because each case is unique, the duration of therapy is determined by the severity of the problem and the patient's rate of improvement.

When it comes to treating aggression and impulse control through applied behaviour analysis, ABA-trained therapists are aware of the attention-related payoff that these behaviours provide for children and teens with relevant disorders, so they are trained to show no external reactions to overt aggressive behaviour directed at them. They also educate caregivers and parents on how to do the same. When confronted with aggressive behaviour, an ABA therapist may advise you to use a response known as neutral redirection instead of punitive measures.

Neutral redirection is a type of applied behaviour analysis that is used to treat aggression and impulse control disorders. It focuses on empowering the caregiver or authoritative figure to handle disruptive and aggressive behaviour in such a way that it is eventually subdued. In extreme cases, if a child with conduct disorder hits a caregiver, they are trained not to react in any way — not even the slightest flinch. They completely demolish the child's attempt to elicit the desired reaction. Neutral redirection teaches the parent, teacher, or caregiver to avoid any reaction and eye contact with the child or teen, implying that they refuse to acknowledge the aggressive or impulsive behaviour. When they are aggressively attacked, their only response should be to remain calm and guide the aggressive child or teen toward more socially acceptable behaviour. Only when the child or teen begins to behave as instructed by the caregiver will they receive attention and direct acknowledgment. Doesn't it sound difficult?

Trying to adjust to showing no acknowledgment or reaction while being aggressively harassed or insulted by a child takes a tremendous amount of self-control.

However, because ABA and its approach are used for more types of conditions than just aggression and impulsivity, it is important for an ABA therapist to understand how individuals learn certain human behaviours and, based on this principle, how it can be changed or altered over time. The therapist begins by assessing the child's or adolescent's behaviour and then develops a treatment plan to improve communication and behavioural aspects that need to be changed for the children or adolescents optimal functioning and development into adulthood. One of the benefits of ABA therapy, as demonstrated above, is that the therapist can train the caregiver, teacher, and adult. However, for this type of therapy to be effective, continuous evaluation and significant measures for effective patient monitoring must be taken. As progression becomes apparent, treatment is adjusted to accommodate and promote further progression.

If you are looking for a qualified and capable ABA therapist, their practice requirements include a graduate-level to a doctorate-level degree, clinical therapist licensure, and additional training and experience in ABA (Psychology Today, 2016; AppliedBehaviorAnalysisEdu.org, 2020).

Family Counseling

Family therapy is a type of psychotherapy that traditionally requires the participation of all members of a nuclear family or a stepfamily, and in some cases, members of the extended family, depending on their relevance to the situation. Family members attend sessions together that are led by either one therapist or a team of therapists with the goal of assisting the family in dealing with or working through issues that are causing dysfunction in the family dynamics and home environment.

Even if only one member of the family has a problem or suffers from an illness, the goal of family therapy is to improve family dynamics. Families may attend therapy sessions together due to the death of a family member, a mental or physical illness, or issues involving children or teenagers such as

ODD. In this case, as in any other where family therapy is used to treat a child or adolescent's disorder, the goal is primarily to work through what causes the family's inability to function normally, and similarly, when a new stepfamily has formed and new family dynamics are in the process of forming. At the turn of the century, therapists began using a new approach known as multisystem therapy, or MST, which is most often performed at the family's home so the therapist can experience the ecological environment of the family being treated. Because a therapist examines how a family interacts within their home environment, MST is often referred to as the "family-ecological systems approach." This approach is particularly useful when there is a problem child or adolescent with behavioural issues or emotional disturbances. MST has been the subject of several clinical research studies, and the general consensus is that it improves family relations, can reduce adolescent substance use and psychiatric symptoms, and can improve school attendance.

Family therapy can be delivered by counselors, therapists, social workers, or psychiatrists over the course of several sessions. A session, for example, would typically last one hour, and these sessions could occur once a week for three or four months.

Here are some interesting concepts related to family therapy:

Patient Identification: The identified patient, or IP, is the family member who is the reason for the family's attendance at family therapy.

This may appear to be blaming the IP, but we are simply stating that because this individual is experiencing specific issues or has been diagnosed with a specific disorder such as ODD, this type of therapy is required and thus attended.

Homeostasis: Homeostasis is a Greek word that means "balance," and it refers to the situation or goal that the family is attempting to achieve through family therapy. The family wishes to restore or address any situations or causal factors that are causing an imbalance in family dynamics, restoring homeostasis or harmonious family life and relationships.

The Extended Family Field: This term refers to the immediate family, the network of grandparents, and other family members. In other words, it is not limited to the nuclear family.

The extended family field also refers to and identifies what is known as the intergenerational transmission of behaviours, problems, attitudes, or emotions. The field can benefit from family therapy that is specifically centered on a child or adolescent, which includes members of the extended family.

Differentiation: This term refers to each individual family member's ability to be their own person while also integrating into a familial community and being a part of a larger whole, which is the family. Thus, a healthy family allows for and accepts individual differences among its members.

Relationships in Triangles: This is a fascinating family relationship theory that is frequently seen in family therapy. According to the theory, when a conflict arises between two family members, they are more likely to enlist the help of a third member to stabilize the situation and maintain homeostasis. Two parents and a child, a parent, a child, and a grandparent, three children, or two children and a parent are examples of typical triangular relationships.

These triangles form as a natural way for a family to maintain homeostasis.

A family therapist will first schedule appointments with family members to conduct a series of interviews in order to provide effective family therapy.

All members of the nuclear or stepfamily are always interviewed, but other members may be interviewed for relevant reasons as well. For example, if an extended family member has a psychiatric illness, the therapist may want to interview this person to determine if there are any other indirect contributing factors. Before the group sessions begin, the interviews allow each family member to provide their version of the issue, and the therapist to get a first impression of each member individually and how they contribute to the functioning of the family.

During these interviews, therapists look for the type and level of emotions expressed by the individual, signs of dominance or submission, the role of each member of the family, how different members communicate, and whether there are any obvious relationship triangles. As part of the preparation, the therapist creates a genogram. A genogram is a type of diagram that depicts significant events and people in the family's history. It may also include medical information and information on major personality traits.

The therapist can use a genogram to identify behavioural patterns that span more than one generation, typical marriage choices, possible family secrets, family alliances, and previous conflict situations, and any other details that may be useful for the specific family the therapist is focusing on.

As a final thought about family therapy, as effective as it can be on its own or in conjunction with other types of therapy, there are times when you should be cautious and consider whether the nature of this therapy is appropriate for the situation you are in. Families with one or both parents suffering from mental illnesses such as psychosis, antisocial tendencies, or paranoia are examples. Another case in point is when a family's inherent cultural or religious values do not recognise psychotherapy or harbor reservations about its practices. A more common example would be a family that is unable to meet regularly enough for effective therapy to be carried out. It's always best to weigh the pros and cons, but family therapy, particularly MST, is an excellent option for children and teenagers with ODD who cause disruption in the home (Encyclopedia of Children's Health, 2020).

Children and Adolescent Psychological Counseling

A child psychologist is specially trained to assist children in understanding themselves from their own point of view. In other words, if a child has a disorder or a mental illness, the psychologist will assist them in determining what is going on in their mind by beginning with their way of thinking and reasoning. Child counseling is for children, adolescents, and teenagers who are suffering from mental disorders or illnesses. This type of counseling is also used to help children who have experienced trauma or a great deal of grief, or who live in a dysfunctional home environment. The goal of child counseling is to break down stressful situations and problems that children face so that they appear more approachable and, eventually, conquerable. Child counseling can greatly benefit your child or teenager if they are trained to see things and communicate things to them from their level and perspective.

Because child counselors are trained to communicate with your child or adolescent on their level rather than trying to lift them to yours, the child may bond more easily with the counselor, a trusting relationship can be established more quickly, and your child is more likely to tell the counselor things about their life and feelings that are important and relevant to their condition but that they would never have revealed under other circumstances.

Child counselors are trained to deal with a wide range of problems that children and teenagers face. These issues include disorders and mental illness, but they also include grief and trauma such as divorce, relocation, the death of a loved one, bullying, sexual or emotional abuse, and addiction or substance abuse in the family. They may also use methods such as cognitive behavioural therapy if they believe it is the best way to treat a child's condition, though their approach may differ slightly due to their specialized training. There are specific behavioural signs that can indicate that your child or teen would benefit from child counseling, according to a child counselor. Urine leakage, unprovoked aggression if the child has significant difficulty adjusting to new situations such as a social situation, academic performance issues if your child experiences constant and excessive anxiety, a sudden disinterest in previous hobbies and activities, addiction or drug abuse, self-harm, or hearing voices are examples of these.

If you believe your child requires this approach, you can consult with a child counselor to see if your child will benefit from this specialized mode of communication (Langham, 2019).

Psychiatry

Because there are no FDA-approved medications for oppositional defiant disorder in the United States, drug treatment is not considered the first best option. Having said that, there are specific drugs that can "rewire" the brain and improve the symptoms of ODD in children and adolescents. When children with ODD were given low doses of atypical neuroleptics like Abilify (aripiprazole) and Risperdal, their behavior improved (risperidone). Medication, on the other hand, should not be considered a primary option due to the scarcity of approved medicinal substances (Rodden, 2017).

Homeopathy

Some people believe that ODD can be treated with homeopathic remedies, while others are opposed to psychiatric medicine due to its numerous side effects.

Homeopathy is a lesser-known treatment option for ODD.

Let's take a look at what homeopathy is, how it can help your ODD child or teen, and which ones are recommended.

Homeopathy is a medical science that considers the physiological and psychological components of an individual in relation to how the disease in question has evolved in the body or mind during the diagnostic process. This concept is employed, and all of these factors are taken into account when prescribing a homeopathic remedy. A homeopath believes that by using this method, they are more likely to discover the underlying cause of an illness or disorder, whereas a medical doctor only looks at the physical and a psychiatrist focuses on pharmaceutical drugs, while their remedies remain natural.

Given these facts, it is safe to say that homeopathy follows a holistic approach.

A homeopath will keep a record of your physical ailments, including undiagnosed complaints, physical and psychological characteristics, and the emotional state you are in during the consultation. This method makes it easier for the practitioner to find the root cause of an issue by viewing it holistically, and it allows the patient to get rid of any thoughts that have been bothering them, as these thoughts will also be deemed important by the homeopath.

In contrast to psychiatric medicine, homeopathic remedies are considered safe, have no side effects, and are in their natural form. Homeopathic remedies have also been shown to boost the immune system and increase energy levels. Homeopathic medicine seeks to balance the psychological, biological, and emotional issues or disturbances that a child experiences when suffering from ODD, thereby improving the child's behaviour. Homeopathic medicine also claims to keep an ODD child from having a relapse, which is a recurring episode that occurs after the child begins treatment. The child's mind can be stabilized and positive behaviour can begin to develop by using homeopathic medicine. Homeopathic medicine is patient-oriented, which means that the medicine prescribed is based on the characteristics of the patient rather than solely on the symptoms of the condition. As you can see, the recommended medications include characteristics that are not typical of ODD. Here are three instances:

CINA: This remedy is especially effective for irritable, anxious, or restless children. The child is also petulant, dissatisfied, angry, and dislikes being touched. The child is extremely demanding and will refuse anything that is offered to him. These children are also prone to being overweight and having a voracious appetite.

NATRUM MURIATICUM: A treatment for children who are easily offended, impulsive, and abusive to others.

This remedy can also be beneficial if a child is malnourished or lacking in vitamins.

TIMONIUM CRUDUM: This remedy is specifically for children who are overly angry and abusive to others. The child is moody, frequently ignores people who speak to them, and is easily irritated. They appear to be angry for no apparent reason and crave attention (Welcome Cure, 2020).

As you can see, these remedies are extremely specific and may contain unusual information about the person whose treatment is being sought. In homeopathy, however, there are more than 50 different remedies used to treat Oppositional Defiant Disorder, whereas there are only two in psychiatric medicine. Will your child fit the profile of one of those fifty treatments? It's an intriguing methodology, and the experience could be healing for the soul.

Home ODD Care

One of the most difficult aspects of living with an ODD child or adolescent is distinguishing their violent and disruptive behavior from who they are as a person because they are not their disorder. They are children or young adults who require guidance and affection. Because you usually associate people with the way they behave, it is extremely difficult to suddenly stop doing it, especially if it is your own flesh and blood. Here are a few pointers to help you manage and stabilize an otherwise chaotic household.

To begin, avoid reacting to or engaging in a power struggle with your child or teen. If you have an ODD mother, you know that this is something they do frequently, and you can quickly dismantle the potential conflict situation by refusing to take the bait. Another way to keep a steady boat is to choose which battles to fight and which to avoid. There will be plenty of provocation and opportunistic attempts at conflict, for example, but some will be more serious than others. Is it necessary to respond to a provocation if it is not serious?

The concept of not reacting does not imply that you should always ignore your child, but you can respond in a non-confrontational manner that shows them that you are willing to pay attention but are not available for fighting about frivolous things.

Then you know they'll break them, but it's critical to establish and enforce clear rules in the home and make it clear that breaking a rule is unacceptable. An ODD child or teen will rebel against this structure, but without a clear household structure, you are not providing a good example of how to live their life. Having said that, you should also give your child the opportunity to express themselves through innocent play. Enjoy these moments of healthy expression with your child or teen if you can.

Even if you have a lot of questions, try not to bombard your child or teen with them. If they appear to want to talk, they are demonstrating a desire to communicate, but you have this handy little guide for any general information about ODD you may require.

Do not rely on or expect your child to explain the disorder to you, as this can be taxing on them.

Help your child establish a routine so that they have something to fall back on when things don't go as planned. This may seem strange because ODD children and teens appear to want to destroy routine and authority, but there is a way to suggest it to them that will have them slip into it without even realizing it. Routine can be like a walking frame for someone with a mental or mood disorder when every limb in their body feels like it doesn't want to move. The trick is to introduce a sense of routine without appearing authoritative, which can cause a reaction or an episode (Mauro, 2019).

Chapter 11
ODD and ADHD

Sometimes a child's defiance is caused not only by ODD but also by ADHD, which may turn out to be the primary cause of their challenging behaviour.

How can two disorders coexist? And how do you know if your child has both? Let us investigate.

The Distinction between ODD and ADHD

You now have a good understanding of the oppositional defiant disorder, but many children who exhibit extreme forms of disruptive behaviour may also have a co-occurring disorder.

Although not every child with attention deficit hyperactivity disorder is diagnosed with an oppositional defiant disorder, several children with ODD also have ADHD.

Despite the fact that there is no medical treatment for ODD, a child with both disorders will benefit from behavioural modification techniques as well as medication to alleviate symptoms.

When your child exhibits symptoms of ODD, your clinician may suggest a comprehensive mental evaluation. Once ODD has been diagnosed, your doctor may recommend a test period during which your child will be required to take ADHD medication to treat this specific disorder, which may actually improve ODD symptoms.

Frustrated or Hot Blooded?

A child with ADHD may become irritated as they struggle to deal with frustrations or educational obstacles. It may appear to be an expression of rage or arrogance. Children with ODD have temper tantrums when they are denied something they desire. Their behaviour is completely deliberate, whereas a child with ADHD did not think about their actions beforehand.

Are you impulsive or aggressive?

As previously stated, children with ADHD "do first and think second." They are prone to impulsive behaviour, and these children are not malicious. Children with ODD intentionally act out. A child with ADHD may push a classmate down the slide because the child is in their way, whereas a child with ODD may push a child down the slide because the child is in their way. If a classmate is injured, your ADHD child will feel terrible about their actions; an ODD child will believe they have won the battle.

Is it inattention or defiance?

In both disorders, parents will give instructions, but their children will not listen. The behaviour is the same, but the reasons for the behaviour differ. An ODD child acts defiantly on purpose because they do not want to follow the rules of any authority figure. They purposefully refuse to cooperate. A child with ADHD hears you but is completely distracted and forgets what you said very quickly if they are distracted by something else. It is not willful disobedience.

Relationship Difficulties

Both disorders cause social isolation and friendship problems. A child with ADHD has difficulty making friends because they misinterpret people. They interrupt people and speak without thinking, which may accidentally upset their peers. They are socially awkward.

Children with ODD intentionally push people away. They enjoy inflicting emotional and physical harm on others. They will intentionally start fights and arguments and will lie without conscience.

What are the Signs and Symptoms of ADHD and ODD?

ADHD and ODD symptoms can manifest behaviorally. The motives of the child are completely unrelated. Fortunately, many

Children with ODD will outgrow these characteristics before they reach adulthood adolescence. Medications will help with ADHD, as well dealing with

ODD symptoms such as depression may also improve.

However, these disorders may progress into conduct disorders.

- that may last throughout adolescence or even when they reach adulthood
- Mature any healthcare provider should pay close attention to all patients.
- signs, symptoms, and causes of both ODD and ADHD
- disorders before making a final determination

If you've noticed that your child's actions are becoming more spiteful or you must be deliberate rather than emotional or impulsive.

Consult your primary care physician for a referral to a mental health/behavioral specialist.

If your child's cognitive and behavioural activities show signs of

In both conditions, it is possible that these ailments are running concurrently.

Both disorders must have signs and symptoms for a diagnosis.

A proper diagnosis can only be made after a minimum of six months.

Symptoms of ODD

- Shifting the blame
- Easily irritated and offended
- Dissatisfaction with authority figures
- Refuses to follow rules
- Loss of temper or being easily irritated
- irritates or shocks others on purpose
- nefarious and venomous
- ADHD Symptoms
- Concentration problems
- Constant fiddling
- Interfering with discussions
- Easily perplexed and disorganized
- Unfocused
- Items are frequently misplaced.
- Inability to take notes at school

Failure to recall daily school projects or other obligations

- Talking too much
- Blurring responses
- Difficulty paying attention to and following instructions
- What is the Cause of ADHD and ODD?
- The initial cause of these disorders is unknown, but we do know
- Genetics and environmental effects are two of the most important.
- reasons for creating them There are several symptoms of
- hereditary disorders and may include types of behaviour that cause
- about self-mutilation or bodily harm Other signs and symptoms include
- hostility and difficulty controlling one's impulses
- Environmental factors also play a significant role in both disorders and
- massive, continuous physical tyranny, negligence, or
- The primary causes of these conditions are corporal punishment.

Many of the characteristics and behaviours associated with ODD may be outgrown in children.

A rebellious adolescent may mature into a laid-back adult. Others, however,

Hostility, for example, could develop into a long-term problem.

Diagnosis of ODD and ADHD

There is no specific evaluation to identify ADHD or ADD.
ODD. A psychological, as well as a medical examination, is required.

- Discard any other possible causes, such as depression or an infection.
- Before a proper diagnosis can be made, there must be an educational deficiency. A youngster
- can have both disorders while displaying only a few symptoms, so an
- The expert will need to investigate their family and personal history, as well as
- consult with educators, childcare providers, or other individuals
- on a regular basis interact with It is critical that you learn the
- treatment options suggested by your doctor

Treatment Alternatives

A dual diagnosis, such as ODD and ADHD, typically necessitates both medical and therapeutic treatment. Medications can help with physical and mental symptoms like restlessness and inattentiveness, while counseling and therapy can help with defiant behaviour modification. Family therapy combined with social skills training is another treatment option for improving communication between parents and children. Cognitive problem-solving skills aid in the correction of negative thought patterns, as well as social skills training methods for learning how to relate to others. When ODD children pose a risk to themselves or the community, hospitalization may be necessary, which may be involuntary for a period of 72 hours for medical observation if necessary.

The Relationship between ODD and ADHD

According to Attitudemag.com, nearly 40% of children with ADHD are also diagnosed with ODD. Specialists believe that ODD is linked to the lack of impulse control associated with ADHD, whereas children with ADHD exhibit oppositional features associated with ODD, even if their defiant behaviours are not intentional. The same article also proposed that ODD is a type of coping mechanism for ADHD-related feelings of frustration and emotional hurt.

Treatment Options for ADHD and ODD

- The right medications can help control your child's ADHD symptoms.
- Behavioral modification techniques will ensure a better demeanor.
- Children with severe behavioural and mental issues should see a qualified family therapist and go through a full psychological screening for other disorders such as anxiety, bipolar, and depression.

Conclusion

You've probably never heard of this disorder, or if you have, it was most likely through a news article. It is a moderately uncommon type of oppositional defiant disorder (ODD) in which the child displays unusually high levels of defiance and anger toward authority figures (i.e., parents and teachers) while also demonstrating low levels of compliance with those same authority figures. However, while ODD is a collection of symptoms characterized by the child's typical passive-aggressive defiance and rebelliousness, it is not a typical case of ODD.

The circumstances surrounding these children's defiant behaviour, in particular, appear to be circumstantial; for example, an argument with the parent causes the child to become angry. If the anger does not manifest itself in an outburst or action, such as hitting or breaking something or collapsing in front of others, it may not meet the criteria for the oppositional defiant disorder (ODD). As a result, the child in question may be experiencing atypical cases of ODD, or even some form of bipolar disorder.

Although the concept of oppositional defiant disorder (ODD) has been around for a long time, it is not widely accepted by doctors or psychologists. However, we have observed some unusual behaviours in children that indicate this possibility, as well as children who fit the oppositional defiant behaviour pattern but do not meet the criteria for ODD. As a result, we developed a list of ODD-related symptoms that cannot be attributed to another condition and can be distinguished from typical childhood defiance and rebellion. These are the symptoms:

- The child is consolable (the child is capable of calming down and becoming complacent after an episode of defiance).
- The child does not engage in self- or other-directed outbursts (i.e., the child does not lash out when defiant but remains calm).
- The defiance is not limited to one area but is visible in all (such as tantrums, anger, rigidity, and belligerence)

- The defiant behaviour is only observed with adults and never with peers.

Surprisingly, we have also observed children who appear to have bipolar disorder but exhibit some of the same symptoms as an oppositional defiant disorder. The following are typical bipolar disorder symptoms:

- The child has manic or hypomanic episodes (i.e., euphoria, increased energy, and a sense of self-importance).
- These are also common times for the child to show defiance and anger toward authority figures (including parents and teachers)
- This defiance is restricted to one area — what the child wants versus what others want.
- The defiance and rage are irreconcilable.
- The best way to distinguish between bipolar disorder and oppositional defiant disorder is to create a "profile" of the child's mood, behaviour, and activity level over the previous several weeks. If you have these symptoms for an extended period of time with no noticeable changes in mood, activity level, or behaviour, you are unlikely to have bipolar disorder. Similarly, if the child is extremely upset on another day but then calms down relatively quickly and returns to normal with no other days above baseline (i.e., typical), this is consistent with bipolar but not ODD.

It's also worth noting that depressed children can develop megalomania, the belief that they can do no wrong and are always correct. Parents and teachers are typically viewed as the outside source of authority in these children. The child displaying oppositional defiant behaviour may also feel entitled to their demands (i.e., make all the decisions, boss everyone around, etc.).